W9-BZG-939

SETTING CONDITIONS FOR CREATIVE TEACHING

IN THE ELEMENTARY SCHOOL

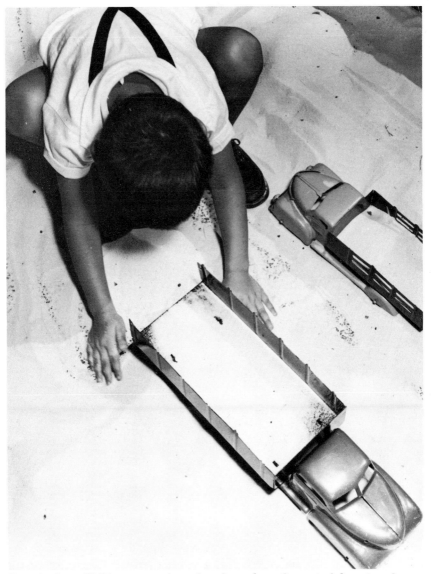

Frontispiece: Children create by using themselves, the materials nature has supplied and the tools Man has supplied.

SETTING CONDITIONS FOR CREATIVE TEACHING
in the elementary school

_____James A. Smith_____

State University of New York
at Oswego

Foreword by

E. Paul Torrance

ALLYN and BACON   BOSTON

Library of Congress Catalog Card Number: 66-14156

Printed in the United States of America

Seventh printing . . . June, 1972

——Foreword

MANY exciting, potentially powerful, and valid educational ideas
have gone unused or have been forgotten altogether because no one
has translated them into practical methods, instructional materials,
textbooks, and the like. The idea of creative teaching has been
among them. Creativity has been a persistent and recurrent issue
throughout the history of education. Actually, the idea of creative
ways of teaching has never had a very good chance to prove its
worth. Teachers and educational leaders have continually struggled
to understand the nature of creative functioning, the conditions
that facilitate and inhibit creative growth, and the means of rewarding creative achievement. Bit by bit, advances have been
made, and in recent years efforts to add to this kind of knowledge
through research and experimentation have been accelerated. We
need to know a great deal more than we do, but in my opinion we
have made enough advances to make possible a more creative kind
of education than has been known up to now. This is why imaginative, informed, and hard-working translators and creative synthe-
sizers like Professor James A. Smith and his associates, who have
created this series of books on setting the conditions for creative
teaching and learning, are such a welcome asset to the educational
enterprise.

The task of retooling — inventing and testing methods, creating tests and instructional materials, devising evaluation procedures
and creating textbooks and methods of teacher education — for
any new educational idea is enormous. It takes tremendous energy,
creativity, courage, commitment, and willingness to risk on the
part of many people. The inauguration of this series of books on

creative teaching is a major venture for Professor Smith, his associates, and Allyn and Bacon. In the past, the adoption of new and improved educational ideas has been retarded by two powerful forces — teacher education institutions and textbook publishers. The case of Braille writing for the blind is an excellent example. Even after Louis Braille had perfected the method of writing that bears his name and had tested it successfully for five years, it was not adopted by schools for the blind. Opposition came from the training institutions because teachers would have to master this new way of writing and from textbook publishers because they would lose their investments in the enormous embossed books then used by the blind. It was not until many years after Braille's death that his method of writing for the blind was adopted.

Innovations in education are usually hailed as "fads" that will soon be forgotten. This is a common expression of resistance to change. Rarely, however, are valid and worthwhile innovations really forgotten, if they are translated into tested methods and materials. Braille had created an alphabet, a way of writing, that had been taught successfully to blind children. The idea of Braille writing could be rejected but it could not be forgotten. Similar statements might be made about the educational innovations of people like Socrates, Froebel, Montessori, and others. They created and tested methods and materials that have been rejected for a time, but the world has not been able to forget them. Many people have said that the idea of a more creative education is a fad that will pass and soon be forgotten. It *is* possible that creative ways of teaching may be rejected, but they will not be forgotten. Professor Smith and his co-authors in this seven-volume series have in a variety of ways expressed the definition, the spirit, and the truths of creative teaching in a way that will be difficult to forget.

The format of each of this seven-volume series illustrates concretely many of the most important principles of creative teaching. Through the format and structure of these books, the author and publisher recognize the reader as self-acting and stimulus-seeking. The reader is provided both the guidance and the freedom necessary for creative growth. These books are a rich source of ideas, but this is not their greatest value. The reader who uses them for rapid reading or for occasional reference will miss an important opportunity for personal growth and professional development in creative directions. The "great ideas" quoted at the beginning of chapters are provocative. The suggested activities preceding most chapters provide worthwhile explorations in creativity. The content of the chapters provides a wealth of information that translates research findings into classroom methods and instructional materials. The exercises and questions at the end of each chapter will help the reader to make a creative synthesis of these experiences.

The authors offer themselves as models of creative teaching. They bring to their task the fresh aroma of first-hand experiences in creative teaching in the college and university classroom and in elementary schools. They also offer the reader a variety of other models of creative teaching, making him feel almost as though "he were there." Participation in the experiences of the authors and the teachers they have observed, however, is not enough. The authors have added to this the kind of guidance that helps the reader identify, understand, and generalize the important principles at work in these experiences. This should increase the chances that the reader will develop useful skills and be able to transform his own classroom behavior.

Each of the seven books has its own unique contribution, along with a consistent philosophy. Book I is a creative synthesis of Professor Smith's rich experience in teaching children and teachers of children, a vast amount of research concerning creativity and classroom learning, and his theories of education. It is far more than this, however. The author has gone beyond all of these and, building onto the contributions of others added his own innovations. He has distilled a great deal of the essence of the creativity of children. Book II, *Setting Conditions for the Creative Teaching of Language Arts in the Elementary School*, is a comprehensive, well-organized, and rich source of ideas. Book III, *Setting Conditions for the Creative Teaching of Reading and Literature in the Elementary School*, is perhaps my own favorite. It is interesting and exciting and assumes a positive and consistent position on important issues in teaching reading. It will be difficult for the reader to resist becoming a creative reader. The way in which the author heightens expectations and challenges the reader to do things with what he reads is quite compelling. The books on social studies, science, the arts, and mathematics have their own unique features and should be valuable in courses on teaching methods in these areas and to teachers in service who want to become more skilled in setting the conditions for creative learning.

It is my own hope that your creative use of this series of books will help you realize more fully your own dream of helping your pupils live more creatively. This is the challenge of our day. In the past, we have been able to survive with static goals and concepts. This is no longer true. Things are changing so rapidly that our civilization can no longer survive if we insist on thinking and living in static terms and returning to the "old ways."

E. Paul Torrance

University of Minnesota

to
DOT
PAT
and
SUE

Two roads diverged in a wood, and I
I took the one less traveled by,
And that has made all the difference.

———————————Robert Frost

──Preface

IN *recent years, an insatiable interest has developed in the creative process. Much of the interest has come with the realization of the value of the creative mind to the democratic way of life. It is an essential characteristic of the democratic way of life that each individual counts. It is an accepted democratic principle that each individual should receive equal opportunity to develop his potential. It is a known fact that the mechanized and technological age in which we live makes puppets of many men, rather than thinking, contributing and creative members of a democratic society. In factories and on the assembly line, the brains of Americans have been set to idling while the hands of Americans have automatically performed the menial tasks necessary to assemble an automobile or a TV set. America cannot afford such a wanton waste in brainpower. America, standing on the threshold of the space age, cannot afford to lose one single mind that idles because of lack of stimulation and use. A whole society suffers when minds become strait-jacketed into narrow channels of thinking. Such minds resist new ideas, become selfish and self-centered and inhibit progress. Industrial leaders, alarmed over the human robots they have produced, are seeking to find ways to release the creative energy locked in the minds of their workers. Scientists seek perpetually and almost frantically for ways to approach the problems of the space age. Politicians work desperately at finding creative ways to meet world problems. In all phases of life today, the need for new and fresh ways of solving problems is apparent. Creativity has become a precious commodity. The schools must play a substantial role in producing this commodity in the citizens it turns out for the democratic way of life.*

What is creativity—this precious commodity? Can the school develop it in each child?

When we speak of creativity today, it is not with the same meaning that we gave to that word thirty years ago. We speak of creativity today in terms of the heretofore unsuspected creative potential of all men: the ability of each individual to produce with originality, the emergence in various forms of an innate ability found in every human being.

We know the potential for creative thinking is there. Our problem is to find the way to release it: how to set conditions for developing this precious human resource.

That is what this author has attempted to do: write a series of books which show how to set conditions for drawing out the creative potential in youngsters. That is what creative teaching is: the setting up of situations in such a way that each child is stimulated to create. It is helping every child to identify so closely with a problem at hand that tensions are created which make him search through his past experiences for solutions to the problem, and finding no exact solution, rearrange his experiences and come up with new ideas and new solutions. In teaching creatively the teacher instigates creative situations. In responding to these creative situations, youngsters create new ways of dealing with their problems.

To help the reader to understand more fully the creative process and how it can be translated into creative teaching, the first book of the series discusses the nature and nurture of creativity as it is currently understood. The content of this book is culled from the research in this area, the current thinking of scholars on the subject, the author's demonstrations with children and his observations of the work of creative teachers.

The remaining books of the series translate the basic principles of creativity into methodology which demonstrates how creative teaching differs from other types of teaching, and produces different results. These books bear the following titles: Setting Conditions for Creative Teaching in the Language Arts; Setting Conditions for Creative Teaching of Reading and Literature; Setting Conditions for Creative Teaching of the Creative Arts; Setting Conditions for Creative Teaching of the Social Studies; Setting Conditions for Creative Teaching of Mathematics; *and* Setting Conditions for Creative Teaching of Science.

The series is designed so the first volume in the series may be combined with any or all of the other volumes to make a comprehensive picture of teaching for creative development in any area of the elementary school curriculum.

Basically, many of the ideas on the pages of these books may be considered instructional procedures which develop creativity by placing the learner in life-situations where he solves problems, however simple or complex, that are within the realm of his own experience. They are approaches to learning that have encouraged or prompted children to become creative thinkers and doers. In and of themselves they will probably not produce creative teachers, but they will release creativity in children. And it is unlikely that the teacher who gets the "feel" of teaching by creative techniques could ever have received the same satisfaction from the overly-structured, overly-dominated classrooms of the past where creativity was a by-product rather than a basic objective.

Many teachers are sharing their ideas with you in these books. But you will violate the very concept of creativity if you try to use them as cookbooks. Copying in any form is a contradiction of the creative act. Creativeness follows no set pattern, but comes from the innermost being of each individual. This is not to say that you should not try the ideas from these books in your own classroom. Do so by all means! But every time you use an idea, ask yourself, "What ideas do I as a creative person have that fit my particular group," or "What ideas do my children as creative people have that I could use to develop that creative ability?" No, these are not cookbooks of recipes designed to add an ingredient here or there to a human being to be baked in the oven of time and turned out as a creative person. These books are to be considered more as a stimulus to creative effort whereby children may find out what it means to become masters of their own creative powers, and teachers become the challenging, creative individuals so needed in our complex modern world.

These books have been written with two groups of teachers in mind: the college students in teacher education who are looking forward to fulfilling their own creative role in our society through means of creative human relationships in teaching, and the teachers in service who are seeking ideas for enriching their own work.

Throughout the series, reference has been made, for the most part, to unidentified teachers in the feminine gender. I took this liberty because the majority of the teachers whom I observed were women, and it was more comfortable writing about them in this manner.

I am indebted to many people for the material in these books. First of all I am indebted to the children with whom I worked and with whom I tried my own creative ideas. Secondly, I am indebted to the hundreds of teachers who sent me material, who allowed me to visit their classrooms, and who granted me the privilege of working with the children in their classrooms. I am deeply grateful to many of my own students who helped make this manuscript suitable for use in college classes.

James A. Smith

Contents

Contents

Contents

PART
ONE

THE NATURE
OF
CREATIVITY

*A*ctual creativity I define as the process of bringing something new into birth. *This distinction is between art as artificiality on the one hand and true art on the other. It is a distinction that artists and philosophers have struggled to make clear all through the centuries. Plato, for example, put his poets and his artists down in the sixth circle of reality, because, he said, they deal only with appearances and not with reality itself. He was there referring to art as the frosting of life in contrast to the real food, art as decorative, a way of making life prettier, a dealing with semblances rather than with reality itself. But in his later beautiful dialogue, the Symposium, he described what he called the* true artists, *namely those who bring into birth some new reality. These poets and other creative persons are the ones who express* Being itself, *he held. Or, as I would put it, these are the ones who enlarge human consciousness. Their creativity is the most basic manifestation of man's fulfilling his own being in this world.*[1]

—ROLLO MAY

[1] Rollo May, "The Nature of Creativity" in *Creativity and Its Cultivation*, ed. Harold H. Anderson (New York: Harper & Brothers, 1959), p. 57.

I——What Is Creativity?

WHO AM I?

I have many things I want
   to say but—
Noone will listen.

I have many things I want
   to do but—
Noone will let me.

There are so many places
   I want to go but—
Noone will take me.

And the things I write
   are corrected but—
Noone reads them.

Who Am I?

—Jody
Age 8

THIS poem was placed on my desk one day by a third-grade boy of high intelligence who attended a school in an above-average socioeconomic suburb.

Jody was quiet and withdrawn, one who never volunteered in class discussions, and I was delighted at his creative efforts. But more particularly, the content of his poem made me take a fresh look at myself. I felt it to be an indictment against all the adults who had ever worked or played with this child.

For he was insisting that he had something to say about his life and how it should be shaped, that "attention must be paid." I realized that, in our rush to amass new knowledge and pass it along to children, we have forgotten that such knowledge is significant only to the degree that a child can take it and use it to fashion his own place in the sun. All people realize their potential largely through the contributions they make, rather than by what they receive. Jody's poem is thus an expression of the individual's desire to realize his potential.

For years the American public school has had as one of its major objectives to perpetuate the knowledge, skills, and values of the culture in which it operates. It has trained children to memorize, to think critically, to see relationships, and to build concepts in terms of this culture. These skills are in the nature of convergent thinking processes: gathering facts in order to arrive at the most likely answer or the most correct answer. As late as 1960 every commercial test on the market, with the exception of the Rorschach Psychological Test, was concerned with measuring convergent thinking processes.

Since the middle '50's attention has been focused on another kind of thinking process: that of *divergent thinking*. Here, facts, concepts, understandings, and skills are put to new uses, and a *new* answer is devised, rather than a likely or correct answer. It is this type of thinking that is the basis of creativity in individuals.

Up until 1955 most of the literature on creativity was largely philosophical, with only a trickle of research articles available on the subject. The accepted belief among most educators was that creativity was an intangible quality, found only in a few people, which could not be researched. It was often called "talent" and creative people were thought to be different or queer. Little was known about the divergent thinking processes or about the manner by which creative talent was developed. Our intelligence tests, such as those designed by Binet, were supposed to measure giftedness in children, but creativity is a kind of giftedness and these tests did not identify creative children. The difficulty lies in the fact that all the items in the Binet tests deal with convergent thinking principles; every test designed since the Binet test has been validated against it. Consequently, the I. Q. test has continued over the years to measure only convergent thinking processes.

If it is the function of the school to develop all aspects of the child's intellect, then educators must turn their attention to those areas of the intellect which develop divergent thinking processes as well as convergent thinking processes. By so doing, they will help to produce the creative people so much needed in the world today.

In 1954 J. P. Guilford[2] of the University of Southern California aroused some interest in research in this area. Since that time, and particularly since the launching of Sputnik, interest in creativity has launched hundreds of studies, hundreds of articles, and numerous books on the subject. It can no longer be said that fruitful research cannot be done on creativity.

The purpose of this volume is to cull from the research and writing in the area of creativity those thoughts which best explain, in physical, philosophical-physiological, intellectual, social, and emotional terms, the process of creativity. We shall then translate this knowledge into a set of basic principles and ideas which can be used to develop creativity as part of the elementary school educational program.

The remaining volumes of this series will show how each area of the elementary school curriculum can be used to develop the processes of divergent thinking and creativity. Each illustration is taken from an actual classroom situation where the author or some of his teacher-colleagues worked with children and observed notable differences in the creative output of the children. It is hoped that teachers everywhere will come to realize that creativity is something every person possesses, and that in reading this series of books, they will come to see that this great force within them can be released, for every teacher has the potential of becoming a creative

---

[2] J. P. Guilford, "The Nature of Creative Thinking," *The Meaning of Creativity Research Bulletin* (Kutztown, Pa.: Eastern Arts Association, 1954), pp. 5–9.

teacher. Through creative teaching, every teacher may help Jody to find out who he is, where he is going, and how he can get there.

A DEFINITION

Many attempts have been made to define creativity. The most common of all acceptable definitions is the most simple: *Creativity is sinking down taps into our past experiences and putting these selected experiences together into new patterns, new ideas or new products.*

Many researchers and experts on the topic of creativity would elaborate extensively on this simple definition but as a frame of reference for the materials presented in this set of books, this definition will suffice.

In a paper presented to the Special Seminar on "Identification of Creativity in Teachers and Students: The Creative Personality," at the ninth annual Creative Problem Solving Institute at the State University of New York at Buffalo, Donald W. MacKinnon elaborates on this simple definition in this manner:

> . . . As I see it, true creativity fulfills at least three conditions. It involves a response that is novel or at least statistically infrequent. But novelty or originality of thought and action, while a necessary aspect of creativity, is not sufficient. If a response is to lay claim to being a part of the creative process, it must to some extent be adaptive to, or of, reality. It must serve to solve a problem, fit a situation, or in some sense correlate with reality. And, thirdly, true creativity involves an evaluation and elaboration of the original insight, a sustaining and developing it to the full.
>
> What I am suggesting is that creativity is a process which has a time dimension, and which involves originality, adaptiveness, and realization. It may be brief as in a jam session of a jazz band or it may involve a considerable span of years as was required for Darwin's creation of the theory of evolution.[3]

Dr. MacKinnon's elaboration of creativity adds depth to the simple definition above. Some authors will argue that creativity must be beneficial to mankind and that this factor should be in-

[3] Donald W. MacKinnon, "Identification of Creativity in Teachers and Students: The Creative Personality." A paper presented at the Ninth Annual Creative Problem Solving Institute, State University of New York at Buffalo, June 24–26, 1963 (mimeographed).

cluded in the definition. To be of value to mankind, creativity must be of a positive nature. There is such a thing as negative creativity. Emotionally disturbed people can be creative but their creativity does not always assume positive outlets. Consider the methods of torture used in ancient times, the techniques employed by Hitler to change the political face of the world, or the methods of violence used during the Civil Rights demonstrations: many of these ideas were truly creative in design but did not benefit mankind in the long run. For the sake of clarity, it is best to concentrate on positive creativity in a discussion of elementary teaching.

MISCONCEPTIONS ABOUT CREATIVITY

Many misconceptions abound about creativity and a word must be said to clarify the author's stand on these issues.

CREATIVITY AND PRODUCTIVITY

In our world of change we tend to regard the *quantity* of production as the unique factor which makes our way of life possible. Productivity implies quantity, whereas creativity implies quality. Once a creative idea is developed, it is often subjected to mass production so more people may benefit from the idea. Good examples of this are: colored television, reproductions of famous paintings, directional blinkers on automobiles, and stereo recordings of great compositions.

Creativity is often confused with productivity in other ways. A symphony orchestra or a ballet dancer is not creative when either is trying to reproduce a composition or a dance exactly as it was presented at a previous time. Reproduction in this sense is a technical process—and the players and dancers at this moment are technicians rather than creators. To be creative means to break away from tradition and do something that is unique, original or different. The *interpretation* which an orchestra director gives to a piece of music may be creative, or the interpretation given in a dance may be creative, but a performance which merely imitates the original presentation is not. Both may give a great deal of pleasure to the audience, but it must be made clear that there is a definite difference between creativity and production.

[5]

The creativity of any given society gives it its impetus for change. It is its productivity which effects the change.

CREATIVITY AND THE FINE ARTS

For years the fine arts have been viewed as the media by which creativity can be expressed. Art, music, drama and literature can claim the greatest creative output of all the areas of endeavor in this country. This is probably because creative endeavor has been more readily accepted by the public in these areas, and more creative people have directed their output into these fields. But creativity can be developed in all aspects of living, and consequently, in all areas of the elementary school curriculum.

Ghandi's attempt to secure gains for India through fasting is a good example of a creative idea by which a man gained political recognition without violating his philosophy of non-violence. He created an idea that would arouse, not the anger of man, but his compassion. The first sit-down strike might also be classified as a creative idea. Role-playing is a technique often used in business, education and industry to help people understand each other's viewpoints and feelings. As such, it may also be a creative idea.

Science has long been considered a highly technical enterprise. But scientists are among the most creative people in the world today. Not only do they sink down taps into the past experiences of mankind, they must also hypothesize what will happen if they put together ideas which have never been tried before. The launching of the first rocket into outer space was a venture accomplished by many creative scientists and technicians. Discoveries or inventions of this nature are the most creative of all for they are new not only to the individuals involved, but also to the world.

CREATIVITY AND TALENT

Creativity is often considered a God-given quality possessed by a chosen few. But creativity is not a given talent. It is often identified as talent because something in our current plan of education and our present mode of living kills it off in so many people. Chapter II will discuss this aspect of creativity more thoroughly. It is important to understand that creativity is somewhat akin to love: the capacity for it is present in all people at birth. The environment into which it is placed determines to a great degree whether or not it develops to its fullest potential.

CREATIVITY AND THE LEARNING PROCESS

Teaching for creativity, especially as it has been developed in the fine arts, has often been considered a "frill" in the American public school curriculum. Recent research into creativity has helped to dispel this misunderstanding by showing that: (1) creative learning is a highly effective way of learning and (2) "frills" are a necessary part of the teaching-learning process if progress in educational practices is to be made.

Concerning the first point, there is substantial evidence to show that children often learn more effectively and retain longer what they learn through creative learning processes. The creative learning process employs all those facets of learning which have been considered essential to the learning act—and more.

Secondly, "frills" must be considered the vanguard of educational advancement, the area in the educational process where new ideas are being put to test. These tests may result in sound outcomes that will, in turn, produce profound changes in educational methodology, classroom organization and learning procedures. In this sense, "frills" may be regarded as necessary for educational advancement. Hence, rather than a "frill," creative teaching and learning may well be the core of the educational process.

SUMMARY

Research into creativity has alerted educators to the fact that the development of divergent thinking has been grossly neglected in our schools up to the present time. Now that divergent thinking processes have been identified as the base of creative production, schools can make a significant contribution to the development of creative powers in all children.

Creativity may be simply defined as sinking taps into our past experiences and putting these selected experiences together into new patterns, new ideas or new products. Creativity implies quality of a unique nature. It can be developed through all areas of the elementary school curriculum. All people have it to some degree. Creative learning may be the basic core of all learning.

To the College Student

By the time you have finished reading this chapter you will have an awareness of creativity. Look for it around you and list evidences of creativity as it appears in your classmates. Note some of these things:

- The manner in which your classmates dress—the common elements of their dress in their desire to conform to the group and yet the individuality of each student as he tries to be himself.
- The manner in which your classmates seek to be individuals in class contributions.
- The manner in which they live in their sorority and fraternity houses or dormitories. In most dormitories the rooms are alike or are constructed around one basic design. Yet as you walk from room to room, are you more aware of the likenesses of each room than of the differences?
- A new housing development where all the houses are alike. After two years have passed is this still so? Notice how the individuality of people has asserted itself in each house: added wings, paint, shrubbery, added entrances, porches, and decorations.

Keep a record of times you observe creative teaching in elementary classrooms or in your college classes, and compare them with instances of non-creative teaching. Analyze these instances to the point where you can list some characteristics of creative teaching against non-creative teaching.

Think of an elementary school teacher you once had whom you have never forgotten, because she or he was such a good teacher. Why have you remembered this person as a good teacher all these years? Would you say that creativity entered into the picture in any way? What other qualities did this person have? What qualities make a good teacher?

To the Classroom Teacher

Select some children in your class whom you feel are particularly creative. Try to analyze their activities to justify your choice.

Notice all the ways you can in which the individuality of the children in your class breaks through: their clothes, the way they speak, the way they react to stimuli you provide, the way they write, paint and draw. Think of all the ways these individual differences are an advantage to the classroom program.

Think through your daily schedule and check all the times your children are required to conform. Then think through the times they are allowed to be creative. Is there an unbalance in any one direction? Is this good?

Plan to do one thing in your classroom which you have never done before. Try this every day for a week. Ask yourself if trying a new idea each day provided motivation for the children? For yourself?

To the College Student and
the Classroom Teacher

Here are some common exercises which tend to show whether people are creative or not. See if you can do them:

(1) Draw 4 straight connecting lines with a pencil through each of the dots below. You cannot lift the pencil from the paper once you have begun.

(2) OTTFF _ _

The above pattern of letters makes sense once you gain insight as to their relationship. If you gain this insight you will be able to add two letters to fill the last 2 blanks. Copy this problem on a 3 x 5 card and set it on your desk so you will see it at least once every day. If you figure out the solution, write on the back of the card when and where the solution came.

Make a list of "technical artists" often referred to as "creative artists."

Think of five people who lived in the past whom you feel were very creative: artists, architects, poets, doctors, etc. Read something about them. Qualify your choice.

Take a strip of colored scrap paper. Examine it carefully and then make a list of all the things you can think of that you can do with it.

SELECTED BIBLIOGRAPHY

Anderson, H. E. (ed.). *Creativity and Its Cultivation.* New York: Harper and Row, 1959.

Anderson, H. H. "Creativity and Education," *AHE College and University Bulletin*, XIII, No. 14 (May 1, 1961).

Andrews, Michael (ed.). *Aesthetic Form and Education: Syracuse Symposium Conference on Creative Arts Education.* Syracuse: Syracuse University Press, 1958.

Barkan, M. and Mooney, R. L. (eds.). *The Conference on Creativity: A Report to the Rockefeller Foundation.* Columbus, Ohio: Ohio State University Press (Multilith).

Carpenter, R. "Creativity: Its Nature and Nurture," *Educational Leadership*, LXXXII (1962), 391-95.

Dunkel, H. B. "Creativity and Education," *Educational Theory*, XI (October, 1961), 209-16.

Eisner, Elliot. *Think With Me About Creativity: Ten Essays on Creativity.* Dansville, N. Y.: F. A. Owen Publishing Co., 1964.

Follett, M. D. *Creative Experience.* New York: Longmans Green, 1924.

Getzels, Jacob W. and Jackson, Philip W. *Creativity and Intelligence.* New York: John Wiley & Sons, Inc., 1962.

Guilford, J. P. "The Structure of Intellect," *Psychological Bulletin*, LIII (1956), 277-95.

————. "Three Faces of Intellect," *American Psychologist*, XIV (1959), 469-79.

———— et al. *A Factor-Analytic Study of Creative Thinking. I. Hypotheses and Description of Tests.* Los Angeles: University of Southern California, 1951.

Landis, Mildred A. "Creativity, A Precious Possession," *Childhood Education*, XXXVII (December, 1960), 155-56.

Lowenfeld, Viktor. "Current Research on Creativity," *NEA Journal*, XLVII (1958), 530-40.

Maslow, A. H. "Cognition of Being in the Peak-experiences," *Journal of Genetic Psychology*, XCIV (March, 1959), 43-66.

————. *Motivation and Personality.* New York: Harper and Row, 1954.

Mearns, Hughes. *Creative Power: The Education of Youth in the Creative Arts* (rev. ed.). New York: Dover Publications, 1929.

Murphy, Gardner. *Human Potentialities.* New York: Basic Books, Inc., 1958.

Osborn, Alex F. *Applied Imagination* (rev. ed.). New York: Charles Scribner's Sons, 1963.

————. *The Creative Education Movement.* Buffalo: The Creative Education Foundation, Buffalo, N. Y., 1965.

Rugg, Harold. *Imagination: An Inquiry into the Sources and Conditions that Stimulate Creativity.* New York: Harper and Row, Publishers, 1963.

Smith, James A. *Creativity: Its Nature and Nurture.* Syracuse: School of Education, Syracuse University, 1964.

Taylor, Calvin W. *Creativity: Progress and Potential.* New York: McGraw Hill, 1964.

————— (ed.). *The Third Research Conference on the Identification of Creative Scientific Talent.* Salt Lake City: University of Utah Press, 1959.

Taylor, Calvin W. and Barron, Frank. *Scientific Creativity: Its Recognition and Development.* New York: John Wiley & Sons, Inc., 1963.

Torrance, E. Paul (ed.). *Creativity.* Minneapolis: University of Minnesota, Center for Continuation Study of the General Extension Division, 1959.

—————. *Guiding Creative Talent.* Englewood Cliffs, N. J.: Prentice-Hall, Inc., 1962.

—————. *Rewarding Creative Behavior.* Englewood Cliffs, N. J.: Prentice-Hall, Inc., 1965.

Von Fange, E. K. *Professional Creativity.* Englewood Cliffs, N. J.: Prentice-Hall, Inc., 1959.

Wertheimer, M. *Productive Thinking.* New York: Harper & Brothers, 1945, 1959.

Wilt, Marion E. *Creativity in the Elementary School.* New York: Appleton-Century-Crofts, Inc., 1959.

Zirbes, Laura. *Spurs to Creative Thinking.* New York: G. P. Putnam's Sons, 1959.

*T*he great lesson to be learned from evolution is the continual emergence of new kinds of organisms. That man has arisen from the beasts is surely important to know, and that all living things are related to one another by virtue of a common ancestry; but the distinctive feature of the evolutionary process is that it brings forth both biological novelties—new forms, types, and patterns hitherto unknown on earth and (still more important) holding promise of greater changes yet to come. Organic evolution is as truly a creative process as the one described in the first chapter of Genesis and the seventh book of Paradise Lost.[1]

—EDMUND W. SINNOTT

[1] E. Sinnott, "The Creativeness of Life," in *Creativity and Its Cultivation*, ed. Harold H. Anderson (New York: Harper and Brothers, 1959), p. 13.

II——The Physical Nature of Creativity

EVERY child is born with some creative potential, though there is a wide difference in degree. Each individual can be compared to a canvas on which an artist works: the form is the same but every touch of the brush on this canvas changes it into something different from any other canvas in existence. From a time before birth, so is it with a child: his genetic inheritance and the effect of environment and personalities upon him make him different from any other child in the world. Whether or not the creative ability within him will remain alive depends almost completely on the kind of world in which he finds himself and the people with whom he associates.

Because the combination of genes and the cluster of experiences for each individual is unique, and because creativity stems from biological and environmental sources, it cannot be considered as a precious gift inherited by a few lucky people. Everyone is creative to a degree, even though a high order of intelligence is necessary for highly creative acts.

Viktor Lowenfeld, the art educator, has this to say about children:

If children developed without any interference from the outside world, no special stimulation for their creative work would be necessary. Every child would use his deeply rooted creative impulse without inhibition, confident in his own kind of expression.[2]

Allen Dow, the architect, makes this contribution:

Knowing that the human being is such an individual physically, it must follow that his thinking apparatus is also individual. With this view in mind, I fail to see why we cannot assume that each person is by nature a creative personality. Rather than worry about how to make him more creative, we should take this quality for granted.[3]

ALL CHILDREN ARE CREATIVE

All children are creative—of this I am convinced. My recent work with children has made me more and more aware that it is impossible to predict where creative talent can be found. It is everywhere: among the slow-learning, the brilliant, the average, the privileged and the culturally deprived. The greatest satisfactions I have ever received in my life have come in the past four years in working with all these types and trying to set loose the creative force among them. It is always there—and if I am creative enough to set the proper conditions it breaks through, often in the most unexpected places.

Take Marlee, for instance. Marlee was in a class of slow-learning fifth graders in a culturally deprived, slum area of a large central New York city. Like her classmates, her only playground was the dirty streets which surrounded her home: streets lined by crooked, dilapidated houses. Marlee's teacher had challenged me to find anything creative in any one of these children—most of whom came from broken, poverty-stricken homes.

In this particular lesson I was trying to build a good, expressive oral vocabulary with the children, using whatever contrived or

[2] Viktor Lowenfeld, *Creative and Mental Growth* (New York: MacMillan, 1947), p. 1.

[3] A. B. Dow, "An Architect's Views on Creativity," in *Creativity and Its Cultivation*, ed. Harold H. Anderson (New York: Harper and Brothers, 1959), p. 30.

natural situations I could that would relate to their own experiences. We were looking out the school windows at the houses across the street. They seemed to crowd in on us, with their grayness, their dirtiness and their crookedness: but they were their homes and I thought we might arouse some good "feeling" words from discussing them. Across the front of one old gray house grew a magnificent vine. It was fall and the vine was flame-red. We discussed the beauty of the vine and found words to describe it. We then discussed the beauty of the old, gray wood and the contrast it afforded to the bright colored vine. We then began to think of other words to describe the houses. We talked of what made a home, and words like love, security, family, happiness, togetherness appeared on our list on the board.

Marlee had said nothing during our discussion. Finally, I said to her, "Marlee, do you want to add something to our list of words to describe the houses across the street?"

"Yes," she said in a tone of defiance, "they are *ugly*!"

"Oh." I said, "Why do you feel they are ugly?"

"Because," she said, "my father has taken me out to visit my uncle in the country and out there the houses are all pretty and white or green or pink—and there is grass and trees and flowers—and lots of sky and birds. But these houses—they are ugly!"

I allowed the children to discuss the word ugly and added it to our list, but went on to talk about the beauty that came from relationships within the home and not just its outward appearance. Finally I told them I felt they had so many good words on the chalkboard and so many good ideas, I would very much like to see them do something with them on paper. Would they write to me about "The Pictures Across the Street," "The Window Picture," "The Red Vine," "Old Houses," or any other topic they preferred.

Here is what Marlee wrote:

THE UGLY HOUSES

Every day I walk to school
I walk between two rows of
   ugly, gray houses.
Every day I walk to school
And the houses get grayer
   and uglier,

> Every day I walk to school
> The ugly, gray houses get
>   nearer and nearer.
> If I don't get out of here soon—
> They will fall in on me
>   and smother me.

The spelling and punctuation were poor but the diction was not! And what therapy this child received in being allowed to express her feelings this way!

Another day I was in a school in a culturally deprived area. These were not slow-learning children: they were heterogeneously grouped in a fifth grade and had an excellent teacher. She had invited me in to see for myself what sharp youngsters they were and to help her think of more ways to release their creative energies.

I made my visit a week before Valentine's Day and set conditions for creative writing by taking fluorescent chalk and a black light. These children had never seen black light or fluorescent chalk, which is white like any other chalk in regular daylight.

I asked them if they would like to make a magic valentine with me. They were eager to try and wanted at once to know how it would be magic. I told them that would be a surprise. I drew two large hearts on the board and allowed each to select a piece of fluorescent chalk from the box I passed around. Working by twos, they came to the chalkboard and each drew something on the hearts I had drawn to make the magic valentine. As soon as a third of the class had drawn their ideas on the valentine, I asked them to help me to find words and ideas that would describe our valentines. The ideas poured forth: one valentine was frilly, lacy, soft, dainty, romantic, lovable, cool, beautiful, handsome. The other was bold, striking, romantic, cracked, sad, unhappy, uncomfortable. Before I could suggest it, one child said, "I have an idea for a poem"—and we were off—

> We drew two hearts in two
>   different places.
> We dressed them up with
>   arrows and laces

> —and so forth

By the time the hearts were decorated the poem was completed. I asked them if they would like to say it together so I might hear it and added that perhaps we could put it on tape. I asked for suggestions as to *how* we might say it as a choral poem. Hands were up and flying—ideas came at me from right and left. We decided to follow Carolyn's suggestion: that each person who had contributed a line be allowed to say his line and the class would echo it as a chorus.

This was done and the children were delighted with the results.

Then came the moment for the magic. I snapped on the black light under the chalkboard, Paul pulled down the shades and I asked the children to all say the magic word "Abracadabrah" as Peter snapped out the lights to completely darken the room. Such gasps of surprise and delight as the valentines shone in a multitude of colors! We then had to explain how the black light worked— and each had to experiment with the chalk.

"Now," I said, "let's think of ways we can describe this experience to other people. We will have to be very careful to choose good words and put them together into good ideas so people who were not here today will really understand what happened. Let's share some of the ideas that you have in your own heads."

Again, the hands were flying. The ideas tumbled forth—ideas I could not have imagined because I did not have the imagery of these children.

"We gasped with delight," they said.

"It was like a gorgeous broken rainbow," said Carolyn.

"A firework's valentine," said Bruno.

One little fellow whose name was Jack had been very noticeable all afternoon. He was skinny, with big ears and an undernourished body. But he was energetic and his hand was up and waving every time I asked a question. His teacher told me he lived in an old house in the slum area that had been made over into several apartments. He was one of five children, and his entire life had been spent in that limited environment. Both parents worked and he often had to get his own meals and get himself ready for school. As far as she knew he had no enriching experiences except for an occasional trip to the neighborhood movie theater and to the assemblies provided by the school. Yet this child had maintained a zest for living. He responded with enthusiasm to every stimulus

I presented. Here is a list of some of the ideas he gave me about the magic valentine.

"It glowed with fluorescent beauty."

"The valentine was a symphony of color blends."

"When the lights went out, I was dazzled by the beauty of the burning colors."

"We all gasped with delight, so it was delightful."

I lauded Jack and said, "Here is a boy who could some day be a poet. Do you ever write poetry, Jack?"

"Yes," he said, "I love to write poetry."

"Keep it up." I encouraged, "keep it up."

After they had written to me about the valentines I introduced a box on which I had put a label "Beautiful Junk." In it I had placed odds and ends I had collected: a piece of bleached wood, an old bunch of artificial grapes, a worn piece of red velvet cloth, a discarded toy reindeer, a bright pink satin bow, a sparkling stone. I challenged them to think of unique words to describe each particular object—words which applied to *this* object more than to any other. As I drew each from the bag, I placed it before a piece of colored cardboard and set each along the window sill. Here are some of the things Jack said:

About the grapes: "They are tears of wine."

About the deer: "It is springy with life."

When I placed the purple grapes before a yellow cardboard background, he said: "Speaking of color blends, Mr. Smith, you just created a beautiful color blend when you put that bunch of purple grapes in front of that yellow paper. Boy, that really makes them show up!"

And later, "Mr. Smith, I don't want to tell you what to do, but you could make a better color blend along the window sill if you would put a yellow cardboard, then a black, and then a yellow rather than two yellows and a black, the way you've got it now."

One of the greatest thrills in all my work with children came that afternoon when at 3:15 I packed my materials to leave. All the children wanted to help—they crowded around asking if they could take my things to my car. I dispatched some of them to my car, each loaded with boxes, baskets and the tape recorder. When I had said goodbye and thanked them and was about to leave, Jack met me at the door. His eyes were sparkling and he held out his hand to shake hands. "I hope you will come again," he said. "And, Mr. Smith, I'm going to keep up with my poetry!"

My files are full of exciting things children have said and done in the most unlikely places and at the most unlikely times. On the day of the magic valentine, Carolyn wrote:

TWO VALENTINES

Such lovely, pretty Valentines,
  On the board they looked so fine.
There they were, right in their places,
  Dressed up nice with rosy faces.
Then all of a sudden they came alive!
  It was amazing!
  They were ablazing!
Oh beautiful, delightful, so lovely were they!
  Just like the beautiful flowers of May!
So gorgeous, tremendous! Oh, lovely they were!
  There were so many colors it was all a blur!
  Two lovely Valentines!

—Carolyn Butler
Grade 5

Even Othegna, a slow-learning, over-sized, over-aged girl, who had never written anything on her own before, wrote for me:

THE MAGIC VISIT

We had a magic visit today.
It's the sort of thing children will enjoy.
Our visitor was sort of important too; his
  name is Mr. Smith. He taught us about two
  valentines.
First we drew two valentines and decorated them.
Mr. Smith used fluorescent chalk to make the colors
  for his projector.
He turned on the color projector directly at the
  valentines and it was just like magic.
It turned into all different colors like the wonder-
  ful World of Disney. It was really amazing.

[19]

This is all I have to say about him, but we really
enjoyed having him and we hope he makes that magic
visit again.

—Othegna Gethers
Grade 5

I am convinced that all teachers in all situations, be those
situations rich or deprived, brilliant or dull, can keep creativity
alive. But it will come only when we understand what creativity
is and make learning so exciting and full of discovery that all
children will feel "We gasped with delight—so it was delightful."
And to children all learning *can* be delightful!

SUMMARY

All children are born with some creative potential although there
are differences in the degrees of creativity in individuals. Creativity
occurs at practically all ages and in all fields of human endeavor.
It is developmental, and its growth depends largely on the environment in which it is placed and the conditions which nurture it or
thwart it.

To the College Student

Observe all the ways in which your peers show their individuality, especially the many little ways that creativity breaks through in their everyday living such as: individuality in hair styles, selection of clothes, choice
of colors, etc.

Can a parallel be drawn between the creativeness in nature and the
creativeness in individuals?

In the story of Marlee, what *opportunities* did the teacher set up which
made possible the creation of her poem?

Do you feel some of your classmates are talented? What is the difference
between talent and creativity?

[20]

To the Classroom Teacher

Observe all the ways your students show their individuality—in their choice of colors, their expression through painting, their use of words, their play.

Study the lesson about Marlee. What were some of the conditions the teacher set up to make possible the creation of Marlee's poem.

Do you consider creativity something to be added to the current school curriculum or a new way of approaching the teaching of the present school curriculum?

Study the reasons why you feel you are not as creative as some other people you know.

To the College Student and the Classroom Teacher

What evidences do you see in the world about you that creative talent is present in a great many people and to different degrees?

Can you observe any evidence about you which would indicate that creativity deteriorates with age?

Make a list of all the ways you can think of to get students to express their ideas in class.

If possible, watch a nursery school child the first time he encounters a new media such as sand. What does he do with it? Does anyone tell him what to do with it? Is he learning anything by manipulating it? If no one told him what to do, how do you account for his learnings?

What role do you think instinct plays in creative thinking? Empathy? Talent? Experience? Education?

Make a list of ideas you would use to induce students to return books to the library.

SELECTED BIBLIOGRAPHY

Anderson, H. E. (ed.). *Creativity and Its Cultivation.* New York: Harper and Brothers, Publishers, 1959, chap. 2.

Andrews, M. F. (ed.). *Creativity and Psychological Health.* Syracuse: Syracuse University Press, 1961.

Barron, F. "The Disposition Toward Originality," *Journal of Abnormal and Social Psychology,* LI, No. 3 (1955), 478–85.

Christensen, P. R., Guilford, J. P. and Wilson, R. C. "Relations of Creative Responses to Working Time and Instructions," *Journal of Experimental Psychology,* LIII (1957), 82–88.

Dunkel, H. B. "Creativity and Education," *Education Theory,* XI (October, 1961), 209–16.

Foundation for Research on Human Behavior, *Creativity and Conformity,* ed. Carol Lundington. Ann Arbor, Michigan: Edwards Brothers, Inc., 1958.

Gardner, J. W. *Self-Renewal.* New York: Harper and Row, 1964.

Gerard, R. W. "The Biological Basis of Imagination," *Scientific Monthly,* LXII (June, 1946), 477–99.

Gerry, R., DeVeau, L. and Chorness, M. *A Review of Some Recent Research in the Field of Creativity and the Examination of an Experimental Workshop.* Lackland Air Force Base, Texas: Training Analysis and Development Division Project 56–24, 1957.

Moustakas, Carl E. (ed.). *The Self: Explorations in Personal Growth.* New York: Harper and Brothers, 1956.

Osborn, A. F. *Your Creative Power.* New York: Charles Scribner's Sons, 1948.

Reed, E. G. *Developing Creative Talent.* New York: Vantage Press, 1962.

Stein, Morris and Heinze, Shirley J. *Creativity and the Individual.* Glencoe: The Free Press, 1960.

Veatch, Jeanette. "The Structure of Creativity," *Journal of Educational Psychology,* XXVII (1953), 102–107.

*T**he mainspring of creativity appears to be the same tendency which we discover so deeply as the curative force in psychotherapy*—man's tendency to actualize himself, to become his potentialities.[1]

————————————————————————CARL R. ROGERS

[1] Carl R. Rogers, "Toward a Theory of Creativity," in *Creativity and Its Cultivation*, ed. Harold H. Anderson (New York: Harper and Brothers, 1959), p. 72.

III———The Psychological
Nature
of Creativity

ONE September afternoon Marion came running into our fourth grade classroom clutching a dandelion.

"Look what I found as I came across the school lawn," she said, her eyes bright with excitement, "a dandelion! The dumb thing doesn't know it isn't Spring!"

Several of the children gathered around to see the dandelion. We talked about it and I brought out the fact that it seemed more beautiful to us in September than in the Spring because it was rarer. I suggested to Marion that she do something with it so we might all enjoy it for the rest of the afternoon. At first she suggested putting it in a vase, but one child reminded her that it would quickly die because dandelions do not have the same kinds of stems to draw water that other flowers have.

"Why don't you go back to our 'beauty' cupboard," I suggested, "and see if you can find something there to put with it and make a still-life picture."

Just about this time Marcia came into the room holding two more dandelions in her hand.

"Look," she exclaimed, "I found these two dandelions on the school lawn!"

"Good," I said, "Marion also found one and was just deciding what to do with it. Perhaps you two can work together and make us a beautiful still-life picture."

I left Marion and Marcia to their work as I turned to help other children. Soon they were at my desk asking me to come see their still-life picture.

They had pushed an extra desk before the room. On it they had placed a piece of crumpled blue-green burlap. On the burlap they had placed a shallow white vase, washed inside with a soft, blue glaze. In this they had floated the three dandelion blossoms. Around the edge of the vase they had placed an old bleached piece of driftwood which I had picked up one Sunday afternoon on a trip to the seashore.

The still-life was, indeed, very beautiful. As soon as it was time for school to begin, I asked Marion and Marcia to tell about their picture. Then, as was customary in our classroom, we sought for *unique* words to describe the arrangement. We wrote on the chalkboard some analogies for the dandelions:

They look like buttons on a clown suit.

They look like baby chrysanthemums.

They look like exploding stars.

They look like tiny, golden sun bursts.

They resemble golden tassels.

In describing the driftwood, they said,

It looks like a wrinkled old lady's skin.

It looks like twisted arms.

And one child remarked, "It looks like old, cracked, wrinkled fingers scratching at the water."

After we had discussed the still life picture and I had listed many of the children's unusual ideas on the chalkboard, I suggested that they write to me about the dandelions whenever they had time during the afternoon.

At the end of the day a small pile of papers had accumulated on my desk. This is what Marcia had written:

THE DANDELIONS

I walked to school today. I walked across the lawn. I saw two dandelions. I picked them and took them to school. I discovered Marion had also found a dandelion. We put them together in a vase with a piece of driftwood. They made a pretty still-life picture.

This is what Marion wrote:

THE DANDELIONS

I walked across the lawn today.
It seemed to me
Each dandelion became a gold, gold star
On a green, green sea.

A comparison of these two pieces of creative writing brings to mind many questions. Marcia's story was precise, correct but unimaginative and stodgy. Marion's was fresh, imaginative, rhythmical, delightful!

In the last chapter it was pointed up that environmental conditions determine to a great degree whether or not the creative drive in humans becomes actualized. Yet, here are two children, raised in families of the same socio-economic level, attending the same school under the same teacher each year. Yet, in one, the ability to express herself creatively has already been stifled; in the other it still lives. What makes the difference? It is obvious that similar *physical* environment is not the total answer. How do we explain the fact that creative talent *has* been developed in some children while it has not been developed in others? If we had the answer to that question, many of our problems regarding the creative process would be solved.

CONCEPTIONS OF CREATIVE THINKING

In recent years researchers have attempted to explain this phenomenon. So far, most of the literature about this problem is theoretical. Because most of the impetus for research in creativity originates in the theories about creative thinking, it is well to review them here.

Up to this time there are six conceptions of thinking: (1) traditional logic, (2) classical associationism, (3) Wertheimer's Gestalt formulation of productive thinking, (4) psychoanalytic conceptions as formulated by Freud, and as reformulated by Kris and Kubie, (5) dynamic perception theory as stated by Schactel, and (6) Rugg's theory of transliminal chamber.

In the book by Getzels and Jackson, *Creativity and Intelligence: Explorations with Gifted Students*, the authors do an excellent job of explaining the basic premises behind each of these conceptions of thinking.[2]

TRADITIONAL LOGIC

In traditional logic, thinking is concerned with the truth of statements. Getzels and Jackson explain logical thinking as follows:

> Being true or false is a quality of assertions and propositions and only of these. Propositions involve general concepts—class concepts—which are basic to all thinking. On the basis of assertions, inferences are drawn, and certain formal conditions are applied to test whether the inferences are valid. Certain combinations of propositions make it possible to derive "new" correct propositions, and logic establishes the various forms of syllogism which guarantee correctness of conclusion . . . A new branch was added to the system of traditional logic at the time of the Renaissance. This is the procedure of induction with its emphasis on experience and experimentation. The focus here is not on deduction from general propositions but on gathering facts and observing their relationships, which culminate in general assumptions. Syllogisms are viewed as the tools by which consequences are drawn from such general assumptions in order to test them.[3]

CLASSICAL ASSOCIATIONISM

Getzels and Jackson explain the classical formulation of associationism as follows:

> Thinking is held to be a chain of ideas, or, in more modern terms, a chain of stimuli and responses, or a chain of behavior elements. The way to study thinking is to study the laws governing the succession of ideas or behavioral items. An "idea" was held to

[2] Jacob W. Getzels and Philip W. Jackson, *Creativity and Intelligence: Explorations with Gifted Students* (New York: John Wiley and Sons, Inc., 1962) Chapter 3, pp. 77–132.

[3] *Ibid.*, p. 78.

be some remnant of perception, a copy, in more modern terms a trace of stimulations; and ideas or items were connected when they occurred together quite the way a telephone number is connected with a name . . . Habit and past experience—repetition rather than reason—are the essential factors in thinking.[4]

In this system new ideas are the associations of old ideas by trial and error. From the point of view of the theory of associationism, Wertheimer says the ability to think productively is the working of associative bonds and depends on the number of associations an individual has acquired.[5]

GESTALT FORMULATIONS OF PRODUCTIVE THINKING

Wertheimer proposed the Gestalt formations of productive thinking which sharply opposed traditional logic and classical associationism. He said that the thinking process proceeds by the structuring of Gestalten. In this process there is first a problem situation in which the problem starts and the structure of the problem is incomplete. A number of steps lead to the second situation—in which the structure of the problem is completed, the process ends and the problem is solved because the structural trouble has disappeared.

Wertheimer suggests that all productive thinking partakes of these features:

(1) There is *grouping, reorganization, structurization,* operations of dividing into sub-wholes and still seeing these sub-wholes together, with clear reference to the whole figure and in view of the specific problem at issue . . . (2) The process starts with the desire to get at the *inner-relatedness* of form and size. This is not a search for just any relation which would connect them, but for the nature of their intrinsic interdependence. Outstanding relations of this kind—sensible with regard to the inner structural nature of any given situation . . . play a large role here. (3) There is the feature of the functional meaning of parts . . . (5) The entire process is one consistent line of thinking. It is not an and-sum of aggregated, piecemeal operations. No one step is arbitrary, ununderstood in its function. On the contrary, each step is taken surveying the whole situation . . .[6]

[4] *Ibid.*, pp. 78–79.

[5] M. Wertheimer, *Productive Thinking* (New York: Harper and Brothers, 1954), p. 9.

[6] *Ibid.*, pp. 41–42.

Wertheimer points out that in some creative processes (as in art and music) the creator does not start with a problem but, instead, envisions the desire to get at the inner-relatedness of form and size. In this instance step 2 replaces step 1 but the inner structural requirements determine the procedures of the solution of the problem.[7]

PSYCHOANALYTIC CONCEPTIONS

The psychoanalytic and neo-psychoanalytic conceptions of creative thinking were advanced by Freud. He drew a parallel between conflict as a genesis of neuroses and conflict as a genesis of creativity, noting that the forces motivating the artist were the same conflicts which drive other people into neurosis. The unconscious mind is the base of these conflicts and in the unconscious also lies the creative and neurotic solution to these conflicts.

Getzels and Jackson have neatly summarized the Freudian approach to creative activity as follows:

(1) Creativity has its genesis in conflict, and the unconscious forces motivating the creative "solution" are parallel to the unconscious forces motivating the neurotic solution; (2) the psychic function and effect of creative behavior is the discharge of pent-up emotion resulting from conflict until a tolerable level is reached; (3) creative thought derives from the elaboration of the "freely rising" fantasies and ideas related to day-dreaming and childhood play; (4) the creative person accepts these "freely rising" ideas, the non-creative person suppresses them; (5) it is when the unconscious processes become, so to speak, ego-syntonic that we have the occasion for "achievement of special perfection"; (6) the role of childhood experience in creative production is emphasized, creative behavior being seen as "a continuation and substitute for the play of childhood."[8]

The authors go on to point out that a more recent formulation by Ernst Kris has shifted the interest from id processes to ego processes. In this "neo-psychoanalytic" formulation there

. . . is a tendency to shift the locus of creativity from the unconscious to the preconscious; and despite this shift, the special kinship between neurotic and psychotic processes, and creative processes

---

[7] *Ibid.*, p. 195.

[8] Getzels and Jackson, *op. cit.*, pp. 91–92.

is more or less maintained; . . . in effect, creativity is an "act of regression in the service of the ego." As Schachtel says of this attitude toward creativity, creative behavior is seen as essentially "the product of a *repressed libidinal or aggressive impulse* and of a *regression* to infantile modes of thought or experience, to the primary processes, albeit in the service of the ego."[9]

Lawrence Kubie rejects the assumption that to be creative a man must be infantile or sick. He rejects the role of the unconscious in creativity and points out that the role of the unconscious is to warp creativity. He states:

> . . . I believe that it would come closer to the truth, . . . to say that the creative person is one who in some manner, which today is still accidental, has retained his capacity to use his preconscious functions more freely than is true of others who may potentially be equally gifted.[10]

Kubie makes definite distinctions between "preconscious," "conscious," and "unconscious" mental processes. Preconscious processes have the highest degree of freedom in allegory and in figurative imagination. The contribution of preconscious processes to creativity depends upon their freedom in gathering, assembling, comparing and reshuffling ideas. Kubie argues that *both* the conscious and the unconscious processes act in such a way as to rigidify the preconscious process and thus render even the most potentially gifted person uncreative. Kubie also states that the essential quality of the creative person lies in his ability to allow preconscious material readily to achieve conscious expression.[11]

Kubie says in his thesis concerning creativity:

> A type of mental function, which we call technically "the preconscious system" is the essential implement of all creative activity; and . . . unless preconscious processes can flow freely there can be no creativity.[12]

[9] *Ibid.*, p. 94. Also see E. G. Schachtel, *Metamorphosis: On the Development of Affect, Perception, Attention and Memory* (New York: Basic Books, 1959), p. 24.

[10] L. S. Kubie, *Neurotic Distortion of the Creative Process* (Lawrence: University of Kansas Press, 1958), pp. 47–48.

[11] *Ibid.*, p. 37.

[12] *Ibid.*, p. 137.

He suggests that the creative person has a greater "flux" or movement of preconscious material into his conscious expression than the intellectualized person.

DYNAMIC-PERCEPTION THEORY

Schachtel's Dynamic-Perception Theory offers another position on the cause of creative thinking. Schachtel believes that which underlies creative production is the openness of the individual to the world about him—the approach to the riddle of creativity is not through the framework of psychoanalytic theory but through the framework of perceptual theory. Schachtel defines two different ways of communication between subject and object—one subject-centered, or autocentric, and the other object-centered, or allocentric.

Schachtel defines creativity as the "art of seeing the familiar fully in its inexhaustible being, without using it autocentrically for purposes of remaining embedded in it and reassured by it."[13]

In his own words:

> . . . it is the existential struggle between the two tendencies in man: to remain open toward the world, capable of allocentric perception, or to seek the security of secondary embeddedness in a closed world and in the shared autocentricity of familiar perspective.[14]

Creativity signifies the victory of the first tendency over the second. Schachtel states it as follows:

> The man who lives completely in this cocoon has proceeded from the primary imbeddedness in the womb and in the world of mother to the secondary embeddedness in the culture, usually in the subculture of the particular social group to which he belongs. He has proceeded from the primary autocentricity of the infant's perceptual world to the secondary autocentricity of the adult's world of "objects-of-use," in which all objects are reduced to and exhausted by the familiar labels and reactions the culture provides for them. On his way from primary to secondary embeddedness he has passed through a period during which the world seemed open, inexhaustible, exciting, full of wondrous and adventurous possibilities, not to be described by any label. But while the "cocoon" at which he arrived is larger than the womb was, and while within it

13 E. G. Schachtel, *Metamorphosis*, p. 184.
14 *Ibid.*, p. 188.

there are many more objects than the infant ever dreamt of, they have lost their aliveness, just as the man who has "matured" to the state where he does nothing but contribute to the protective uniformity of the cultural cocoon has lost his enthusiasm, his capacity for growth, the essential and specifically human capacity to remain open toward the world, that is, to transcend a closed pattern of reactions and thus to encounter and perceive the new, that which transcends the labels of his "patterned" experience, be it in a new object or in an object encountered many times.[15]

RUGG'S THEORY OF THE TRANSLIMINAL CHAMBER

A recent conception of creative thinking was presented by Harold Rugg in his book, *Imagination: An Inquiry Into the Sources and Conditions That Stimulate Creativity*. Rugg's theory varies from those presented above in several respects.

Rugg contends that all life is lived on a continuum ranging from the conscious to the unconscious. On this continuum there is a critical point at which the mind is free (uninhibited) to draw from either its conscious or its unconscious states. Rugg refers to this point as the critical threshold and it is his thesis that the illuminating flash of insight which is essential to creativity occurs at this critical threshold. He labels this particular point on the continuum as an "off-conscious" stage (as compared to Kubie's "preconscious") and gives this across-the-threshold power a name: "the transliminal mind." It is the center of creative energy.

Rugg does not believe the subconscious lies asleep waiting to be called on at certain times or coming to the fore only in dreams, or in times when the organism is off-guard. He believes the subconscious takes an active vital part in everyday living. Actually, he feels it is the unconscious mind which does most of our thinking. In his own words:

> I have come to think of life as lived on a conscious-unconscious continuum. Six different ways of conceiving human behavior may be brought together on a single continuum. Behavior may be conceived as reaching from conscious to unconscious, from sleeping to waking, from trance state to normal state, from autism to reality, from fantasy to symbol, from inattention to hyper-alert attention.
> . . . If we should emphasize Dewey's theory of problem-solving thinking or that of the logical positivists, we would visualize think-

---

[15] *Ibid.*, pp. 185–86. See also, Getzels and Jackson, *op. cit.*, pp. 116–17.

ing as focused at the extreme conscious end of the scale. The calm thinker, alertly aware, consciously and tensely strives to focus attention on the problem. There is no reference to the unconscious, to the intuitive quiet mind. The stress, on the contrary, is on the active conscious mind. If we should follow Freud's interpretation, we would picture the person moved unwittingly by the unconscious, shaped in his thinking and action by long-forgotten, perhaps repressed, experiences of early childhood. I prefer to locate the creative worker at the critical threshold of the conscious-unconscious border, the transliminal state. In linear terms this is between Dewey and Freud . . .[16]

Rugg's theory differs from Kubie's in one basic way: Kubie ascribes creative ability *only* to the preconscious while Rugg holds that there are creative capacities in all sectors of the continuum.

Kubie and Rugg both indicate that the essential quality of the creative person lies in his ability to draw from as many of life's experiences as possible. Kubie locates creativity in the ability of a person to allow preconscious material readily to achieve conscious expression. Rugg feels it happens when people place their minds in a "transliminal chamber," an area somewhere between the conscious and the unconscious where the mind is free to draw from total life experiences to develop new ideas. The more open the mind to all experiences, or the less inhibited, the greater the possibility of creativity or of preconscious content in the conscious process.[17]

OTHER PSYCHOLOGICAL THEORIES

There are other psychological explanations as to why some children have been able to retain their creativity while others have not. One by Abraham Maslow is well worth considering.

Maslow[18] explains high level creativity in his theory on the order of the basic needs of man. He states his order of needs as follows:

First level: The most essential body-needs: to have access to food, water, air, sexual gratification, warmth, etc.

Second level: Needs that relate to physical safety.

---

[16] Harold Rugg, *Imagination: An Inquiry into the Sources and Conditions that Stimulate Creativity* (New York: Harper and Row, 1963) pp. 42–43.

[17] Getzels and Jackson, *op. cit.*, p. 110.

[18] A. H. Maslow, "A Theory of Human Motivation," *Psychological Review*, L (1943), pp. 370–96.

Third level: Needs that relate to love—to be loved, to have affection, care, attention, and emotional support.

Fourth level: Needs that relate to maintaining satisfying relationships with others—to be valued, accepted, and appreciated as a person; to be esteemed and respected; to have status; and to avoid rejection and disapproval.

Fifth level: Needs that relate to achievement and self-expression —to be creative and productive; to perform acts that are useful and valuable to others; to realize one's potentials and translate them into "actuality."

Maslow feels that children cannot achieve until their first three basic needs are comfortably taken care of. Creativity functions most freely on levels four and five. He feels that the full creative powers of people are released only after they have enough physical and psychological security in life to be free of strong ego involvements.

Maslow's concepts are of major importance to our understanding of school achievement and creative development. Lack of achievement, he is telling us, may very well be due to basic unmet physical, safety and emotional needs. By the same line of reasoning, the creativity in children cannot be developed until certain physical and status needs are met. The attitude of the teacher, then, might be a solid force in killing off creative enterprise.

Picture the kindergarten child who comes to school somewhat insecure and bewildered in his first experience away from home and mother. The teacher is a mother-substitute and he wants security and comfort in his new situation. Assume the teacher understands the creative process and gives him many materials with which to work—and then accepts his products with praise or encouragement. This child is getting status (a kind of love) from the teacher by creating, so he will continue to create.

If, on the other hand, this child should have a teacher who does not understand the creative process and who has preconceived notions about "drawing" and helping him master shapes as part of a "reading readiness" program, she may show disapproval with his exploration and experimentation by the tone of her voice, or with such statements as, "What is *that* supposed to be?" (implying it should be something)—or even by over-praising so he does a repeat performance simply to gain the teacher's approval. In such an instance this child may not move on to the next needs on Maslow's scale—he must have his status need met, so he stays at the place where it IS *met*, never to rise above it.

When the teacher gives praise for originality, ingenuity and "different" ideas, she gives the child status for his creativity, and he stands a better chance of rising above the status need.

Some creativity is present at each level of Maslow's hierarchy, however. People can be very creative in their struggle for survival. They invent ingenious ways of keeping warm, of finding food and may even become inventive in the way they steal food should it be necessary. A mother of a large family in a low socio-economic bracket often is very creative in making over children's clothes, in preparing hamburg in several different tasty dishes throughout the month and in using inexpensive materials to make her home attractive.

Many psychologists of late have theorized that an ongoing development of the individual's potential capacities and talents operates through opportunities for originality and inventiveness, as a supplement to the older concepts of tension-reduction.

AN ILLUSTRATION

The theories of creative thinking and creative imagination outlined above can have tremendous impact on our methods of teaching. There are forces at work in the child's world which seem to exist with the intent of inhibiting his creative growth and development. Among these are (1) closure to life experiences—excessive insistence that the child fit into the predetermined cultural patterns of the world into which he is born and (2) excessive conformity to rules, regulations, methods of thinking, ways of behaving and patterns of living.

Conformity is necessary to some degree in order for a society to exist, but *excessive* conformity and restricted approaches to learning are true enemies to creative development.

There are suggestions here as to how creative teaching differs from non-creative teaching. Contrasting illustrations of teaching seem appropriate in order to illustrate the point.

Miss Arnold is a fifth grade teacher. Part of the curriculum in this particular fifth grade is to develop vocabulary by learning the parts of speech. Miss Arnold's objective was to teach verbs. This is how she went about it:

She asked the children to open their grammar books to page 64. When all were ready, she said, "Today we are going to learn about another part of speech. John, read what it says at the top of page 64 in heavy print."

John read, "Verbs."

"Yes," said Miss Arnold, "Mary, will you read the sentence which follows in heavy print, please?"

Mary read, "A verb is a word of action or a state of being!"

"Good," said Miss Arnold, "now who can give me some words that show action?" Some were given, and Miss Arnold then turned to page 64 again and said, "Helen, will you read the list of words on page 64 which show action?"

And Helen read the list printed in the book, "jump, run, walk, fight, talk, etc."

Miss Arnold then discussed the other part of the definition—verbs as a state of being—and called on Frank to read the list of verbs that showed a state of being—be, is, am, are, was, were."

"Now," said Miss Arnold, "let us see what you have learned. Let's select together the verbs from the sentences printed on page 64 and page 65 in your book."

After the children and the teacher had done this exercise together, Miss Arnold asked them to open their workbooks to pages 82 and 83 and underline the verbs in the sentences printed on those pages. This concluded the lesson.

Now, consider Miss Dawson's approach to vocabulary building and to parts of speech.

Miss Dawson had roughed out a plan for teaching some parts of speech, but on the particular morning when she was to present her lesson nature provided a phenomenon which caused her to change her plans. It was a nasty day; the clouds were heavy and black, and great, uneven gusts of wind blew sleet against the windows of her classroom in a broken unpredictable rhythm.

"How many of you liked walking to school in the sleet today?" Miss Dawson asked the fifth grade class. Many did not but some did. "Why did *you* like it?" she asked of John.

"Oh, it was fun," he responded. "Just as I would bend myself to walk into the wind, it would stop and I'd almost fall flat on my face."

"I know what you mean," said Miss Dawson. "How did the sleet feel on your face?"

The class volunteered many new words and ideas and Miss Dawson continued, "Now this is a *special* kind of wind and rain. It is different from the usual kind we have around here. It is what we call *unique* (and she wrote the word on the chalkboard). A unique or different or special kind of wind should have unique or different or special kinds of words to describe it. Let's try to think of some words that describe *this* particular kind of wind or rain."

The children thought, then hands went up.

"Blustery," said Anna.

"Driving," said Davie.

"Both of these are good words," said Miss Dawson, "but they could also apply to other kinds of winds. Try blowing like the wind, or listen to the sleet as it hits the windows and clap your hands softly to the rhythm it makes and see if we can find more *unique* words to describe it."

The children puffed their cheeks and blew, or clapped softly to the uneven rhythm of the sleet on the windows.

Finally Joe said, "What about 'uneven'?"

"That's a good one," encouraged Miss Dawson.

"It is a *grouchy* wind," said Mark.

"Oh, I like that!" said Miss Dawson as she wrote the two new words on the board.

Roberta had her hand in the air. "It is a *spanking* wind," she exclaimed.

"Excellent!" encouraged Miss Dawson. "These are all good words. I think I remember using that word 'spanking' only yesterday—can any of you give me sentences which show how we used it before?"

Soon these sentences appeared on the board:

1. The *spanking* made the boy cry.
2. Marcia *is spanking* her baby doll.
3. He did not like the *spanking*.
4. The *spanking* wind is making our windows cry.
5. The waves were *spanking* the sand.

"Let's look for a minute at all the ways the word 'spanking' can be used as a part of speech," said Miss Dawson.

It was pointed out that in sentence 1 it was a noun used as a subject which they had already studied. In sentences 2 and 5 it was a verb, part of a verb phrase, which they had not studied and which Miss Dawson explained as an action word showing what the subject was doing. In sentence 3 it was a noun used as the direct object which they had studied. In sentence 4 it was an adjective. So, these children learned that the word "spanking" was a word they could use in many different ways to suit their own purposes.

The lesson continued with the children finding other words that could be used in many ways—and labeling them as a part of speech *after* they had been used for effective speech by the children. At the close of the lesson Miss Dawson isolated the verbs from the many sentences which appeared on the board and the children made up a definition for a verb and a verb phrase.

Such a difference in these two lessons! Miss Dawson has provided an open-ended experience where children may feel free to experiment with words and *then* identify them through the accepted nomenclature. She leaves the child's mind in the transliminal chamber proposed by Rugg by refusing to allow unnecessary restrictions to be placed on the use of words. She helps the children put their life experiences into verbal ones by removing restrictions on the use of vocabulary and by giving them free reign to use words effectively. She uses divergent thinking devices—many answers are correct, not just one. She is truly teaching the use of language as a tool, yet she is, at the same time, teaching facts and socially accepted principles without confusing the children. She violates no truths about the structure and use of language.

Miss Arnold's lesson, on the other hand, is a restrictive, confusing one, void of the thrill of discovery and loaded with preconceived conformities, many of which are violations of the truths about language.

In the first place, a definition should come as a result of an experience, not as an introduction to it. Miss Dawson developed a concept and then allowed the children to verbalize it in their own words; Miss Arnold imposed it on them. Secondly, Miss Arnold put inhibiting restrictions on the use of vocabulary when she had the children list verbs—and read the list in the textbook. None of the words listed are verbs in all instances. What about:

He made a gigantic *jump.*
There was a decided *jump* in the graph.

They put the play through a dry *run*.
The woman had a *run* in her stocking.
The *walk* along the lake is lovely in the fall.
I watched the *fight* on television.
We had a regular *talk* fest.

Miss Arnold did not provide the children with the freedom to explore the use of words in many contexts. She did not help the children to discover that parts of speech only become parts of speech *after* they are used in a sentence and that nearly all words can be many parts of speech. She did not point out that assigning a word the label of a part of speech was merely a way of identifying its function in a sentence *after* the sentence was constructed. Children in her class have now had imprinted on their conscious or subconscious minds a list of words which must be used only in certain ways and in particular places in their written expression.

This is one type of teaching which creates the rigid, inhibiting forces that prevent children from becoming creative in their writing. Add to this the restrictive emphasis which Miss Arnold probably puts on punctuation and capitalization and we can see why Miss Arnold's pupils are crippled in their freedom to use vocabulary and why little real creative writing comes from her classroom while it comes in torrents from Miss Dawson's classroom.

SUMMARY

Six conceptions of thinking have been reviewed in this chapter. Later theories of creative thinking differ from the earlier theories in many respects. Early theories relegate creative thinking to the half-mind of conventional psychology. They have been replaced by concepts which consider the part played by the whole mind, both the conscious and the subconscious. Every act of human response is seen as a total integrated response in the new theories. Both intuition and scientific observation and study are seen as ways of knowing and both contribute to the creative act. Creativity is seen as organic, proceeding from the inside out, rather than as mechanistic, proceeding from the outside in. "Felt-thought" rather than verbally-reasoned thought is the crux of the creative act. The creative resources of the mind are viewed as limitless. The human organism can exist only because of the continuity of the tension-release-tension cycle which keeps the mind in a state of imbalance (or aware of incompleted acts). Creativity is fostered by openness to life experiences and problems rather than by memorizing facts and predetermined concepts.

To the College Student

What do you consider to be unnecessary forms of conformity at the college level? List all you can and then categorize them as: administration-imposed, teacher-imposed, pre-imposed, self-imposed. To which of these do you pay most loyal tribute—in other words, which classification exerts the most pressure to keep you from becoming more individual? Can you explain why?

Rugg found, in his studies of creative people, that many people who were ordinarily not very creative were induced to create under hypnosis, under the influence of alcohol or dope, and when they were in a trance-like state. How do you explain this?

If you have an opportunity to read about the Nuremburg trials or see the motion picture, *Judgment at Nuremburg*, do so. Then discuss whether or not the rise of the Third Reich was a creative plan. Read Hitler's *Mein Kampf* and ask yourself whether or not this was a creative plot to gain world power? In light of these readings, discuss the parallel Freud draws between conflict as a genesis of neurosis and conflict as a genesis of creativity.

As you go about your college life, make note of special creative acts that are predominant in their uniqueness, such as:

• A creative television script or a scene on a television program that strikes you as particularly creative.

• A scene from a play that is unusual, unexpected or different enough to be considered highly creative.

• A hair style or costume worn by one of your classmates which is different enough to be labeled creative.

• A section of a book—or a piece of writing which appeals to you as being especially creative.

• A window display with freshness and individuality.

• An unusual scene in a moving picture film.

Share your lists with each other in class, and discuss them. Try to relate the uniqueness of each to the ability of the creator to be unrestricted by preconceived ideas and to keep his mind in Rugg's transliminal chamber—free to draw from all life's experiences rather than just the conscious ones.

Relate, by discussion, the following to creativity:

- illusion
- perception
- imagination
- picturesqueness
- suggestion
- imagery
- symbolism
- conflict
- association
- achievement

Discuss the value of creativity as a positive outlet for emotional tensions.

Do you feel you are autocentric or allocentric according to Schachtel's definition? Justify your conclusions.

The play *Our Town* by Thornton Wilder is a good example of creative theater. Read it with the intent of discussing some of the author's modes of creative expression.

To the Classroom Teacher

Examine your program to see how often during the day you are restricting children's ability to use your teaching in a variety of ways. Think of ways you could change this. For example, are you in a "rut" when it comes to:

- the teaching of handwriting;
- the teaching of phonics;
- the teaching of grammar?
- What about your spelling program? Are children being taught to spell words in your classroom so they can use them in *many situations* or do they learn them to write on a test?

Speaking of tests, can testing be creative? Put your mind in that "trans-liminal chamber" about which Rugg speaks, and come up with a creative idea for your next social studies test.

Rugg feels the flash of insight needed in creativity often comes when the mind is in a semi-conscious state—asleep (in dreams) or in a trance. Just for fun, have your children copy the dot problem at the end of Chapter I on a card, have them take it home to work on it and then ask them to record *when* the solution came. How many were day-dreaming, sleeping, or star-gazing when insight came on this problem? The author gave this problem to a group of adults and ⅔ of them arrived at the answer while driving along the N. Y. State Thruway, somewhat hypnotized by the hum of the car wheels, the monotony of the passing scene and the flip-flop of their windshield wipers.

Try, as many times as possible during one day, to find ways to laud individual or unique products in your classroom and note whether this has any effect in drawing out a greater quantity of individual production.

Consider children in your classroom who appear to be underachievers. What do you know about their backgrounds? Might their underachieve-ment be related to lack of met needs as described by Maslow? What help can you solicit to help meet the needs of these children? Note whether or not they have been able to retain a certain amount of creativity. Can you think of ways to make creativity a way to help them meet these unmet needs?

How many times are you trapped by stodgy textbooks and workbooks into teaching like the Miss Arnold in this chapter? Think carefully about any lessons you have taught recently which fall in this category—what can you do to make them more exciting, more honest, and more produc-tive for the children?

Make a list of the children's books in your classroom which really show creative thinking on the part of the author. Are there many? Few? How would you rate these authors in their ability to use *all* life's experiences as tools with which to create: Lewis Carroll, Dr. Suess, Sir James Barrie.

Ask the children how they like an unusually creative motion picture or story, such as *Mary Poppins, Peter Pan,* or *The Brothers Grimm.* List their reasons—do they recognize the creative elements or are they influenced by other criteria?

To the College Student and
the Classroom Teacher

Using the references given in the footnotes or in the selected bibliography of this chapter, read more about the six conceptions of creative thinking explored here, and decide which one most clearly describes the creative process as it occurred in Jody in Chapter I; in Marlee in Chapter II; in Jack in Chapter II; in Marion in Chapter III.

Make a list of all the unnecessary ways you had to conform during your childhood without ever understanding the reason behind the conformity. How many of these ways (and other ways) are still being imposed on children? What do you consider the value of this kind of conformity, if any?

Conformity of some sort is essential if there is to be a society. Make a list of the forms of conformity children must learn in order to keep the society united.

Design a lesson which leaves children "open to experience" rather than "cut off" from experience.

Read the play *Rhinoceros* by Ionesco. What is its message? Discuss this play and its meaning for the future of the world as it relates to creativity.

Ask yourself "How could we design a classroom and a school program that would most effectively hinder, stifle or kill creativity?" Check your suggestions against your own classroom (if you are a teacher) or the classrooms in which you are observing or working (if you are a student) and note which of these features already exist.

Selected Bibliography

Andrews, M. F. "Experience of Being and Becoming," *School Arts*, XLII (Mar., 1963), 5–9 and (April, 1963), 22–24.

Association for Supervision and Curriculum Development, *Perceiving, Behaving, Becoming*. Washington, D. C.: National Education Assn., 1962.

Getzels, Jacob W. and Jackson, Philip W. *Creativity and Intelligence: Explorations with Gifted Students*. New York: John Wiley and Sons, Inc., 1962.

Kubie, Lawrence. *Neurotic Distortion of the Creative Process*. Lecture Series 22. Lawrence: University of Kansas Press, 1958.

Maslow, A. H. *Motivation and Personality.* New York: Harper and Row, 1954.

Moustakas, Clark. *The Self.* New York: Harper and Row, 1956.

Murphy, Gardner. *Human Potentialities.* New York: Basic Books, Inc., 1958.

Rugg, Harold. *Imagination: An Inquiry into the Sources and Conditions that Stimulate Creativity.* New York: Harper and Row, 1963.

Wertheimer, M. *Productive Thinking.* New York: Harper and Row, 1954.

Zirbes, Laura. *Guidelines to Developmental Teaching.* Columbus, Ohio: The Bureau of Educational Research and Service, Ohio State University, 1961.

*W*ithout passing premature judgment on the possibility of some positive effects from special instruction, we hold that boldness in thinking, free rein to the imagination, and creativity in performance will not be easily forthcoming through piecemeal lessons and artificial stimulants. What is needed is a change in the entire intellectual climate in which we—the parents and teachers —as well as the children function.[1]

—GETZELS AND JACKSON

[1] Jacob W. Getzels and Philip W. Jackson, *Creativity and Intelligence: Explorations with Gifted Children* (New York: John Wiley and Sons, Inc., 1962), p. 124.

IV——The Intellectual
Nature
Of Creativity

THERE is some correlation between creativeness and intelligence. Highly creative acts are performed by highly intelligent people but only a few highly intelligent people are capable of performing highly creative acts.

While high acts of creativity are closely correlated with high intelligence, all humans are creative to some degree, as was illustrated in Chapter III. Much of the nature of creativity as it relates to intelligence has been revealed by the studies of Jacob Getzels and Philip W. Jackson at the University of Chicago and of Paul Torrance at the University of Minnesota.

Early in their research these men found that current I. Q. tests, which are supposed to measure giftedness, did not measure *creative* giftedness. Dr. Paul Torrance has pointed out that to identify gifted children on the basis of intelligence alone, would be to eliminate approximately 70 percent of the most creative.[2]

[2] E. P. Torrance, "Explorations in Creative Thinking," *Education*, LXXXI (December 1960), pp. 216–20.

CONVERGENT AND DIVERGENT THINKING PROCESSES

Guilford,[3-4] in his classic articles on the structure of intellect, contends that intellect can be analyzed into a large number of components which cover a large number of intellectual abilities. He has arranged 120 components of intelligence into his "structure of intellect." He states that there are three ways abilities can differ from each other: (1) content: the areas a person has to deal with which are figural, symbolic, semantic and behavioral; (2) operations: those areas of the mind which have to deal with cognition (knowing), memory, divergent production and evaluation; and (3) products: those areas which deal with systems, classes, relations, transformations and implications.

Creativity fits into this framework as an OPERATION, specifically as DIVERGENT production. This includes such factors as fluency, flexibility, complexibility and spontaneity. Divergent production does not contain *all* the factors which contribute to creative thinking, however. Almost all areas contribute something.

In Chapter I (see page 2 ff) the basic difference between convergent and divergent thinking processes was explained. Both have a role in creative work. A more extended illustration of the contrast between these two types of thinking follows:

A teacher holds a bottle before the class and asks, "What is this?" and the class says, "It is a bottle." This is convergent thinking—one final answer for a question—really a memory question. Convergent thinking may include many such questions and answers used to arrive at the solution to a more complex problem.

But if the teacher holds the bottle before the class and says, "This is a bottle. What are all the things you can think of that I may do with it?" and the answers which follow are diverse, unique or original, such as "You can make a clothes sprinkler out of it; you can fill it with colored sand and make a door stop out of it; you can fill it with colored water and hang it on a string to make a decoration of it; you can store juice in it; you can put a spout on it and make a watering can for house plants; you can paste colored

[3] J. P. Guilford, "The Structure of Intellect," *Psychological Bulletin*, LIII (1956), pp. 267-95.

[4] J. P. Guilford, "Three Faces of Intellect," *American Psychologist*, XIV (1959), pp. 469-79.

papers on it, fill it with sand and make a paperweight from it"—this is divergent thinking. The process requires no one single answer, and the mind is agitated to be more flexible, more searching, more original as the answers are used up, for then answers become more and more difficult.

The sample lesson of Miss Dawson's search for words to describe the rain was a good example of the use of divergent thinking processes.

Originality comes about through divergent thinking. Divergent thinkers do not get into a mental rut. They look at problems differently and in new ways. Once facts are gathered or new experiments performed, they are able to apply convergent thinking. Convergent thinking brings the pieces together and finds orderly, sensible sequential steps to a solution of the problem. The solution to one problem generally opens new doorways to new ideas and new problems. The divergent thinker is stimulated by the new problem and immediately sets to work on it.

Until recently, there were no tests which measured divergent thinking—even though this type of thinking indicates a special kind of giftedness. Reason for the failure of the I. Q. to measure divergent thinking can be explained. The I. Q. metric has been peculiarly immune to advances in our understanding of thinking and behavior because we test the validity and reliability of new intelligence tests against the old ones. In this manner the old conception of intelligence has been perpetuated and it has been sheltered from serious theoretical and scientific investigation.

Academic grades and intelligence tests are, then, poor predictors of creative potential. Also, sheer accumulation of knowledge is no predictor of creativity. There are many people well-versed in the academic fields who have exhibited little creativity.

INTELLECTUAL MEASURES OF CREATIVE TALENT

Guilford has listed the following intellectual characteristics as most likely to be valid indications of creative talent: originality, redefinition, adaptive flexibility, spontaneous flexibility, associational fluency, expressional fluency, word fluency, ideational fluency, elaboration, and probably some evaluation factors.

Dr. E. Paul Torrance[5] has pointed out that the intelligence test does not measure the child's flexibility, originality and depth of thinking intuition. New creativity tests used at the University of Minnesota do measure these traits. These traits identify gifted children as well as intelligence tests do.

Studies of creative children as identified by these tests show that the creative child is often treated along punitive lines by his teachers. His many questions and answers tend to irritate the rigid teacher who often puts him in his place—sometimes before the class—and thereby brings disfavor on the child. The resulting boredom and inability to concentrate may eventually cause such a child to withdraw within himself and a valuable member of society is lost. Dr. Calvin Taylor[6] states that the loss of creative children from the school rolls is greater than the loss of the highly intelligent. Torrance's and Taylor's work implies that teachers tend to favor intellectual giftedness, while creative giftedness is often ignored or stifled because teachers cannot identify it through tests. Torrance indicates that measures of both intelligence and creativity appear to be essential in measuring giftedness.

Characteristics of the Highly Intelligent and Highly Creative

The work of Getzels and Jackson[7] has contributed substantially to our understanding of differences between highly intelligent and highly creative children. Some of the results of their research will aid teachers in identifying and understanding the two different groups.

Their work showed that highly creative adolescents, for instance, were significantly superior in writing stimulus—free themes, unexpected endings, humor, incongruities and playfulness—and showed a marked tendency toward violence in their stories. They tended to exhibit a certain mocking attitude towards conventional "success."

[5] Torrance, *op. cit.*, pp. 216–20.

[6] C. W. Taylor, "Finding the Creative," *Scientific Research*, XXVIII (December 1961), pp. 6–11.

[7] Getzels and Jackson, *op. cit.*

High I. Q.'s tended to be "stimulus-bound" and high creatives tended to be "stimulus-free."

High I. Q.'s were unable or at least unwilling to risk the possibility of being misunderstood, while high creatives did not seem to worry about such risks.

Getzels and Jackson[8] agree that neither I. Q. nor teacher preference identify all highly gifted students. In comparing a highly intelligent group of adolescents with a highly creative group they found: both groups were superior to the general student groups; teachers exhibited a clear-cut preference for the highly intelligent group, with the highly creative group preferred over the general student body; when asked what qualities they would like to possess, the creative group placed high marks, pep and energy, character and goal-directedness *lower* than members of the high I. Q. group and rated a wide range of interests, emotional stability, and a sense of humor *higher* than members of the high I. Q. group. Getzels and Jackson also found that the one characteristic which set the creative group well apart from the high I. Q. group was a *sense of humor*. The high I. Q. group wanted those qualities *now* which they believed would lead to success in adult life. The creative group was more realistic in selecting qualities more related to present aspirations. The high I. Q. group's personal aspirations were closely related to those which the teacher preferred, while the highly creative group showed a slight negative correlation with those aspirations imposed by the teacher and more aspirations toward the self-ideal. In written responses the creative children showed more imagination and originality than the high I. Q. students.

Research studies carried on at the Institute of Personality Assessment and Research at the University of California in Berkeley have also identified some of those qualities and characteristics of the creative person.[9-10] The psychologists working in this study found that there was a high correlation between creativeness and intelligence, although certain creative people score higher on some

[8] J. W. Getzels and P. W. Jackson, "The Meaning of 'Giftedness'—An Examination of an Expanding Concept," *Phi Delta Kappan*, XL (1958), pp. 75–77.

[9] F. Barron, "Originality in Relation to Personality and Intellect," *Journal of Personality*, XXV (1957), pp. 730–42.

[10] F. Barron, "The Disposition Towards Originality," *Journal of Abnormal and Social Psychology*, XLI (1955), pp. 478–85.

facets of intelligence than others. Creative persons have an unusual capacity to record and retain. They are discerning, alert, fluent and have a wide range of information at their command.

Intelligence alone, however, does not insure creativity. Although intelligence is necessary in order to create, above a certain point it does not determine the degree of creativity.

Other findings in research indicate that creative people see relationships well, are capable of using previously learned facts to advantage, can apply previously learned concepts and generalizations to new situations, appear to be able to break down a problem into its constituent parts, to see the relationship of these parts to each other and to be able to apply them to the solution of a problem. Perhaps most important of all, they are able to identify problems skillfully.

CREATIVE THINKING, CRITICAL THINKING AND LEARNING

A great deal of thought has been given to creativity as a thought process and as a way of learning.

There are those who say that all learning is new to the individual, therefore all learning is creative. William Burton[11] however, in *Guidance of Learning Activities* clarifies this concept by stating that learning is more a process of discovery than of creation.

Most learning is problem solving. Ernest H. Hilgard, writing as a psychologist, defines creativity in relation to problem-solving in this manner:

> There have been two major types of approach to problem-solving and creativity. The first of these relates problem-solving to learning and thinking, as a type of "higher mental process" or "cognitive process," to which problem-solving certainly belongs. The second approach, supplementary rather than contradictory to the first, sees creative problem-solving as a manifestation of personality and looks for social and motivational determinants instead of (or in addition to) the purely cognitive ones. It is not surprising that these two approaches deal also with somewhat different topics. The approach via learning tends to emphasize problem-solving in which a high-order product emerges, although not necessarily a highly

[11] William H. Burton, *The Guidance of Learning Activities*, (3rd ed.; New York: Appleton-Century-Crofts, Inc., 1952), Ch. 16.

original one, whereas the approach via personality tends to seek out somewhat more the elements of creative imagination and novelty.[12]

In one of his stimulating articles, Guilford defines four areas of thinking (reasoning, creativity, planning and evaluation) and explores each area. The author concludes that creative thinking, like problem-solving, depends upon different combinations of factors and the combination of factors significant to the task will vary from time to time. He also states that although certain factors such as ideational fluency and originality will carry relatively more weight, other factors not obviously creative may often be significant.[13]

Creativity begins in the mind at a very young age. Very soon after birth, a child shows signs of creative thought processes. He begins to use toys, stones and sticks to depict life around him, and he "plays" out his own feelings through objects which he manipulates and controls. All the time he is thinking, thinking consciously or unconsciously. He thinks about the things with which he comes in contact. He thinks about the air around him, the smells, and the feelings which he has experienced. He asks innumerable questions about these things, and the more he experiences, the more he has the courage to reproduce his experiences creatively with his materials in his play. From an early age his thinking is both creative and critical.

David Russell in his book *Children's Thinking* has differentiated between creative and critical thinking. He says:

> Creative thinking involves the production of new ideas, whereas critical thinking . . . involves reactions to others' ideas or to one's own previous ideas. Critical thinking can be creative in that it creates new insights for the individual, but these insights are concerned with previously established conditions. Creative thinking is very close to the problem-solving process . . . It may be described as "problem-solving plus." Whenever the child or adult puts isolated experiences into new combinations or patterns we may say that creative thinking has taken place and this process does take place in problem solving . . .

[12] E. R. Hilgard, "Creativity and Problem Solving," in *Creativity and Its Cultivation*, ed. Harold H. Anderson (New York: Harper and Row, 1959), p. 163.

[13] J. P. Guilford, "The Structure of Intellect," *Psychological Bulletin*, LIII (1956), pp. 267–95.

The differences between problem-solving or "reasoning" and creative thinking is that problem-solving is more objective, more directed toward some goal, which is usually external. Problem-solving must be more constant with the facts. Creative thinking is more personal, less fixed. It achieves something new rather than coinciding with previously determined conditions. It also tends to involve more intuition and imagination than does the more objective problem-solving, though this difference is clearly a matter of degree rather than kind. The special insights of the scientist, poet, or artist differ only in degree from the insights which all persons use in solving their problems.[14]

Harold Rugg adds a new dimension to the notion that all learning is creative. He tends to feel that all learning and perceptions are, to some degree, part of the creative act. In his own words:

We look for the factors involved in percept-formation in both of the perceiver's worlds—in his inner system of stress and in the external culture. Each individual sees and feels the world in his own way, because each has built a unique body of traces in his organism by having lived his life and interpreted objective events in his own individualistic way throughout infancy, childhood and youth. This amounts to saying that percepts which are traced in the unconscious electrochemistry of the cerebral cortex have been molded by the individual's response to the culture in which he grew up, by that cumulative temperamental and physical development of body and mind which we call life style, and by the dominant wants, purposes, needs which his individual life history has evolved. *Thus perception is much more than imprinting. It is a creative process in itself. The perceiver creates the field from which his percepts, signs and symbols emerge.*

Rugg says that a four-fold flux of percept, motor adjustment, images and concepts is the stuff of the creative mind.[15]

AN ILLUSTRATION

It is appropriate to demonstrate the differences between critical thinking and creative thinking with an illustration.

I recently attended the after-school meeting of a Junior high school class. The advisor had called them together to make plans

[14] David Russell, *Children's Thinking* (New York: Ginn and Co., 1956), p. 306.

[15] Harold Rugg, *Imagination: An Inquiry into the Sources and Conditions that Stimulate Creativity* (New York: Harper and Row, 1963), p. 77.

for the Junior Prom. But they were faced with a serious problem. Because of the failure of a particular money-raising event, they had only $35 in the treasury to use for decorations and refreshments after the orchestra had been paid.

The class president presented this fact to the class and asked what they could do to make the Prom a success with so little money.

The faculty advisor put the group through a brainstorming session wherein they came up with many suggestions about the refreshments to be served. It was concluded that they would take $10 from the $35 to purchase cokes and that each girl in the class would solicit a certain number of people for donations of cookies and cupcakes. That left $25 to be used for decorations.

Now, the gymnasium where the dance was to be held was an old one with a great deal of ugly gymnasium equipment and steel beams exposed to view. In previous years quantities of crepe paper and many screens had been used to create a Prom atmosphere. From records kept by the last Junior class of their expenses it did not appear that this class could do much with decorations to make the Prom the big event of the year. But the class president and the faculty advisor had done some investigating before they called the meeting. They had been promised by the art teacher that they could have two rolls of wide, white mural paper and a large supply of purple construction paper which had been left over from the year's art supplies.

The faculty advisor posed the problem: "We have $25, 2 large rolls of mural paper and lots of purple construction paper. Now, what original ideas do you have wherein you could use these materials and come up with a theme and some handsome decorations for our Junior Prom?"

Soon the ideas began to come:

"We could use a Japanese theme—we could paint Japanese silhouettes on the big sheets of white paper and hang them along the walls to cover them. We could fasten branches to the posts along the sides of the gym and cover them with pink and white crepe-paper cherry blossoms. We could make our own dance programs from the purple paper and put pink cherry blossoms on them. We could use the gym pads for pillows on the floor around the edge of the gym rather than using chairs."

"Or, we could use 'Dances Around the World' as our theme. We could paint silhouettes of all the dances on the white mural paper and hang them around the walls. We could make mobiles of dancers to hang in the middle of the gym. We could make cardboard figures of dancers and fasten them to the poles in the gym. We could make our dance programs to represent dances of each country. We could use card tables around the gym and use small cardboard figures of people dancing the dances of the world on the card tables and on the refreshment table."

These youngsters seemed to spark each other. The class president listed each idea on the board. Soon ten different ideas were listed. The theme they finally chose after a discussion of each was "It's Raining Violets." They decided to hang sheets of the white mural paper around the gymnasium and paint silhouettes of sophisticated dancers on every other one. On the white panels between the dancers they planned to paste enormous violets cut from the large sheets of purple construction paper. From the ceiling they decided to hang hundreds of crepe paper ribbons on the end of which there would be a purple violet. These were to be hung at different lengths to give the illusion of rain. The refreshment table was to be a large lawn umbrella completely covered with purple violets. Strips of cellophane with violets pasted on them would hang all around the table to represent rain. The dance programs would be white with a purple violet pasted on each one. The poles in the gymnasium were to be made into trees, the branches of which would drip cellophane. They planned to place colored spot lights on the dancing silhouettes and the trees. Around the room they planned to place card tables covered with table cloths made of white mural paper and decorated with purple violets. The center of each table was to contain a lighted purple candle. One boy volunteered to bring the record "It's Raining Violets" to play as the Juniors and their guests arrived, and during the intermission.

Here we see an excellent example of creative and critical thinking. The creative thinking came in the brain-storming session where flexibility of thinking, relatedness of ideas, imagination, originality, fluency of thinking, and uniqueness of planning came into play. But, once the ideas were listed, careful evaluation of each was necessary. Which could be done in the time allotted, within the budget allotted, which was the most realistic yet the most appealing, which required the most even distribution of labor, etc.? Facts had to be considered, judgments made, decisions passed. In this phase of the process we see a good example of critical thinking.

As Russell has pointed out, creative thinking involves the production of new ideas whereas critical thinking involves reactions to others' ideas or to one's own previous ideas. Creative thinking is "problem-solving plus."

Whether *all* learning is creative or not may still be a debatable question. The research and literature in this area do seem to point to some accepted conclusions regarding the creative learning process. It can be safely concluded that creative learning is not a stimulus-response type of learning. It is rather a cooperative-experiencing relationship where communication of both thought and feeling is essential.

It is also safe to say that creativity *is* a type of problem-solving stretched along a continuum from very simple thinking and learning to very complex thought processes. At one end of the continuum, a simple problem may be "What color shall I paint the house in my picture?" while at the other end of the continuum a very complex problem which requires a great deal of knowledge, originality, critical *and* creative thinking might be, "How can we place a man on the moon?"

In creative problem-solving the solution offers tremendous satisfactions, not only because a problem has been solved and a job completed, but because the product has aesthetic qualities and the creator has given of himself to the project—something of himself has emerged in a form which he recognizes (and which others recognize) as his own unique contribution to the solution.

SUMMARY

Creativity and intelligence are correlated to some degree. Highly creative acts are performed by highly intelligent people but highly intelligent people are not all capable of performing highly creative acts. Current intelligence tests do not measure creative giftedness in most children. This is because these tests assess mainly the convergent thinking processes of the individual and do very little to assess the divergent thinking processes where flexibility, originality, depth of thinking, redefinition, associational fluency, elaboration, word fluency, expressional fluency, and the other characteristics of creative thinking are developed.

Creative problem-solving is a unique kind of learning which calls for skills above and beyond those required in ordinary problem-solving and critical thinking.

Because of the importance of creativity in the world today, and because of its importance to the self-realization of all individuals, a reexamination of the methodology and curriculum of the elementary school is warranted. If it is the aim of the public school to develop all aspects of the intellect of each child, each ability calls for certain kinds of practice. J. P. Guilford has stated that there has been an imbalance of teaching in our schools toward convergent thinking and very little toward divergent thinking, the components of which develop creative people.

To the College Student

As college students, you are all a select group. There is no one in your select group with a low I.Q. This creates an ideal situation to check much of the findings of research through empirical observation. Each of you make a list for yourselves of the ten most creative people in your class, according to your own opinion. Turn them in to your instructor or to some student and have him select the ten most creative of all the lists of ten. Now do the same thing for the ones you consider to be the ten most intelligent. Compare the lists—how many appear on both lists?

Check the qualities of your class which are possessed by creative people. As an assignment ask everyone to allow himself to write as many ideas for each of the following as he can in 3 minutes. Then share your lists. Do they show spontaneity of ideas, fluency of ideas, flexibility of thinking, originality, redefinition, associational fluency, word fluency, elaboration?

- List all the uses to which you can put a light bulb.
- Write as many sentences as you can containing the word "hot."
- Write as many endings as you can to the following sentence: The brakes would not work so ———.
- List all the games you can think of that you could use at a Halloween party.
- The theme for Spring Weekend is "Storybooks on Parade." Make a list of as many ideas for floats as you can.
- Make a list of unusual yet fitting gifts that you might give to a golfer who has won a tournament.

Make a collection of really creative cartoons, magazine covers, jokes, comic strips, posters and pictures for your classroom bulletin board. These will be the products of highly creative *and* highly intelligent people.

Collect other material which shows the difference between:

- creativeness and cuteness;
- creativeness and sentimentality;
- creativeness and "technical art";
- creativeness and humor or wit.

Is there a difference? Can you define it? Do some of your illustrations contain both of the above pairs? Do some confuse one with the other?

A simple way to see how creative you can be in class is to allow everyone two minutes to interview the person on his left. Then with a sheet of construction paper and crayons, make a composite drawing of the person you interviewed. Remove any threat from the situation by leaving off all names. Have someone collect them and mount them on a bulletin board before the class. Try to guess which person each one represents. Then check them for: creativeness of expression, originality of ideas, variances in technique, amount of content presented and clarity of communication.

To the Classroom Teacher

Check the I.Q.'s of the children in your classroom. What percentage of these would you also rate as highly creative? Which children not on your list would you consider to be creative?

Perhaps the guidance counselor in your school will be interested in identifying the creative children in some of your classrooms. In the book by Getzels and Jackson mentioned in the bibliography at the end of this chapter, the tests on creativity are listed. Also, there are several exercises you might try with your students to check which ones give the most creative responses.

Make a list of the ten children in your classroom who in your opinion are most creative. Check this list with the personality tests given by your school. Did the creative children always have the best adjusted personalities? To be more accurate in your observations, check the list of creative children as identified by the creativity tests suggested in the last exercise with the personality tests. Does the material in this chapter make you feel differently toward the creatively gifted child and his behavior?

Try some of these ideas on your students to see if you can elicit quantity of response, flexibility of thinking, spontaneity of ideas and uniqueness of ideas:

- How many uses can I find for a bottle?

- How can we change the game of Dodge Ball to make an entirely new game?

- How many ways can we show how many 25's there are in 600?

- List all the ways you can think of to make puppets.

To the College Student and the Classroom Teacher

Here are some problems that will develop divergent thinking processes both in you *and* your students. If you are both working in a classroom, try planning some solutions together; then try some with the children.

- List as many ways as you can think of to give book reports so they will develop creative thinking.

- Take a reading lesson from the manual to your basic series and rewrite it so it accomplishes the same objectives but also presents the lesson creatively, or develops creatively, or both.

- Plan a creative physical education period.

- Make a series of circles on a sheet of paper—then fill them in until you exhaust all the ideas you can think of that can be contained in a circle.

- Try the same idea with squares, triangles and rectangles.

- List all the ways you can think of to create musical sounds (such as hitting nails together, jingling glass in a box). Collect some of this material and create a composition. Then, create a way to write it down so you will not forget it.

Make a list of all the creative ways you can evaluate children's progress in your classroom.

Make a list of all the ways you might use an animated cartoon to develop creative thinking among your students.

Make a list of all the ways you might use a film strip to develop critical thinking among your students.

SELECTED BIBLIOGRAPHY

Baker, S. S. *Your Key to Creative Thinking.* New York: Harper and Row, 1962.

Barron, F. "The Disposition Toward Originality," *Journal of Abnormal and Social Psychology,* LI, No. 3 (1955), 478–85.

———. "Originality in Relation to Personality and Intellect," *Journal of Personality,* XXV (1957), 730–42.

Bergson, Henri. *The Creative Mind.* New York: Philosophical Library, 1946.

Childhood Education. *Creativeness and Intelligence,* 39, No. 8. Washington, D. C.: Association for Childhood Education International, April, 1963.

Crawford, R. P. *The Techniques of Creative Thinking.* New York: Hawthorne, 1954.

Getzels, Jacob W. and Jackson, Philip W. *Creativity and Intelligence.* New York: John Wiley and Sons, Inc., 1962.

Guilford, J. P. "The Nature of Creative Thinking," *The Meaning of Creativity,* Research Bulletin. Kutztown, Pennsylvania: Eastern Arts Association, 1954.

———. "The Three Faces of Intellect," *American Psychologist,* XIV (1959), 469–79.

Guilford, J. P., Fruchter, Benjamin and Kelley, H. Paul. "Development and Applications of Tests of Intellectual and Special Aptitudes," *Review of Educational Research,* XXIX (Feb. 1959), 26–41.

Guilford, J. P. *et al. A Factor-Analysis Study of Creative Thinking. I: Hypothesis and Description of Tests.* Los Angeles: University of Southern California, 1951.

Kettner, N. W., Guilford, J. P. and Christensen, P. R. "A Factor-Analytic Study Across Domains of Reasoning, Creativity and Evaluation," *Psychological Monographs,* LXXIII (1959).

Lowenfeld, Viktor. *Creative and Mental Growth.* New York: Macmillan Co., 1947.

McKeller, P. *Imagination and Thinking.* New York: Basic Books, Inc., 1957.

Meer, B. and Stern, M. L. "Measures of Intelligence and Creativity," *Journal of Psychology,* XXXIX (1955), 117–26.

Patrick, Catherine. *What Is Creative Thinking?* New York: Philosophical Library, 1955.

Russell, David E. *Children's Thinking.* New York: Ginn and Co., 1956.

Torrance, E. P. "Explorations of Creative Thinking in Early School Years," *Research Memoranda.* Minneapolis: Bureau of Educational Research, University of Minnesota, 1960.

———. *Highly Intelligent and Highly Creative Children in a Laboratory School.* Minneapolis: Bureau of Educational Research, University of Minnesota, 1959.

————. *Sex-role Identification and Creative Thinking.* Minneapolis: Bureau of Educational Research, University of Minnesota, 1959.

Wertheimer, M. *Productive Thinking.* New York: Harper and Brothers, 1945, 1959.

Wilson, R. C., Guilford, J. P., Christensen, P. R. and Lewis, D. J. "A Factor-Analytical Study of Creative Thinking Abilities," *Psychometrika*, XIX (1954), 297–311.

Wilson, R. C., Guilford, J. P. and Christensen, P. R. "The Measurement of Individual Differences in Originality," *Psychological Bulletin*, L (September 1953), 362–70.

*I*t is now a known fact that nearly all of us can become
more creative, if we will. And this very fact may well
be the hope of the world. By becoming more creative we
can lead brighter lives, and can live better with each other.
By becoming more creative we can provide better goods
and services to each other, to the result of a higher and
higher standard of living. By becoming more creative we
may even find a way to bring permanent peace to all the
world.[1]

─────────────────────────────── —ALEX F. OSBORN

[1] Alex F. Osborn, *Applied Imagination* (3rd rev. ed.; New York: Charles Scribner's Sons, 1963), p. 397.

V——The Social-
Emotional Nature
of Creativity

CREATIVITY IS INDIVIDUALISM

A GREAT deal of legend and folklore have been associated
with the creative person in the past. Creative people
have often been identified as "Bohemian," or "different" or "eccentric." Much of this folklore exists because of misunderstandings about real creativity and
what it is: often individuals or groups of individuals
revolt against conformity and become individualists,
throwing to the winds the accepted values and customs
of their peers. Because many of these people live in
cliques and are associated with artists or musicians
they are considered to be creative and other people
more or less expect them to be different. But these
people are not necessarily creative.

To be creative does mean to be individual. And
to meet individual differences among children, creative
people have frequently designed new plans of instructional organization or new methods of teaching: they
have adjusted materials to the child; they have im-
poverished or enriched the curriculum; they have
altered promotion policies and changed grade stand-

ards; they have homogenized children by ability levels and other criteria; they have introduced the Joplin Plan, the Denver Plan, the Amidon Plan and a score of others; they have ungraded and multigraded schools; they have employed television teaching and programmed learning; they have had core curriculum and unit teaching; they have departmentalized elementary schools, teamed for team teaching, mechanized syllabi, programmed courses of study, used self-instruction, individualized reading, and designed "contracts."

Each of these plans has been successful in a situation where it was carefully applied and evaluated. Many have been a disaster in the communities where they were applied simply because change was held to be important for change's sake and necessary so that a particular school might claim it was in the swim of things.

Despite all our attempts to meet individual differences and develop individual potential, we are still not doing an outstanding job. The reason may very well be that the basic way to help each child become an individual is through the development of his creative powers. In developing the child's creative powers we may find that he is able to meet many of his own needs without all the organizational plans and the gadgets and gimmicks of modern education. For, if children have their creative powers developed within them from pre-school times, even little children may be inventive enough to help themselves more than they presently do (see Volume 4: *Setting Conditions for Creative Teaching in the Social Studies*, Chapter VII). Rigid conformity to an organizational plan may be as detrimental to the development of creativity as conformity to traditional teaching methods.

THE SOCIAL-EMOTIONAL STRUCTURE

OF THE CREATIVE CHILD

In order to identify creative children in our classrooms and to be able to understand how creative people function with other people, we should dispel the folklore which has grown up about these people and turn to some of the research now available about their social and emotional origins and their social and emotional adjustments.

Creativity is more than a set of traits and characters found in a certain group of people; creativity is a whole way of life. Erich Fromm has described vividly how education for creativity is nothing short of education for living:

> . . . Man is always torn between the wish to regress to the womb and the wish to be fully born. Every act of birth requires the courage to let go of something, to let go of the womb, to let go of the breast, to let go of the lap, to let go of the hand, to let go eventually of all certainties, and to rely only upon one thing: one's own powers to be aware and to respond; that is, one's own creativity. To be creative means to consider the whole process of life as a process of birth, and not to take any state of life as a final stage. Most people die before they are fully born. Creativeness means to be born before one dies.
>
> The willingness to be born—and this means the willingness to let go of all "certainties" and illusions—requires courage and faith. Courage to let go of certainties, courage to be different and to stand isolation; courage, as the Bible puts it in the story of Abraham, to leave one's own land and family and to go to a land yet unknown. Courage to be concerned with nothing but the truth, the truth not only in thought but in one's feelings as well. This courage is possible only on the basis of faith. Faith not in the sense in which the word is often used today, as a belief in some idea which cannot be proved scientifically or rationally, but faith in the meaning which it has in the Old Testament, where the word for faith (Emuna) means certainty; to be certain of the reality of one's own experience in thought and in feeling, to be able to trust it, to rely on it, this is faith. Without courage and faith, creativity is impossible, and hence the understanding and cultivation of courage and faith are indispensable conditions for the development of the creative attitude.[2]

In contrast to Fromm's statements, Getzels and Jackson illustrate how the socialization process of life often destroys the creative development of the child. Commenting on Schachtel's concept that the "open" world which should be explored freely by children is turned into a cocoon in which to be imbedded, they say:

> The child learns these "labels" and acquires these "patterned" experiences through the process of socialization. On the one hand, the child learns to renounce, suppress, or redirect drives and impulses that are at variance with proper social standards. On the other, he learns to bring his observed behavior into conformity with the norms and expectations of the society in which he lives. The

[2] E. Fromm, "The Creative Attitude," in *Creativity and Its Cultivation*, ed. Harold H. Anderson (New York: Harper and Brothers, 1959), pp. 53–54.

socialized child has not so much eradicated forbidden inclinations as learned to restrain their manifest expression. It is during the period of socialization that the distinctive pattern of articulation between the deeper and more surface levels of behavior—what will be expressed and what will be suppressed—is established. And it is during this period also that the precise pattern of the manifest behavior is learned. The extent of the inhibition of impulse and the nature of the manifest behavior is a function of the particular standards and child-rearing activities of the groups within which the children are brought up.[3]

The socialization process may give us the masses of nonentities who are neither individuals nor self-realized citizens. The patterns of behavior indicated above may be warning signals that we are over-organizing children and over-conforming them.

Current literature gives us clues as to the kinds of behavior patterns to look for to show that children are still maintaining their creativity. Creative people, for instance, are more sensitive to life experiences and consequently react more fully to experiences with their emotions. Rugg feels this is an essential characteristic of creativity. He says:

> For truly creative work to be done, the drive of passion must be produced . . . there is a solid consensus on the necessity for inspiration, drive, the white heat of enthusiasm for sustained, creative production.[4]

Drevdahl[5] found that creative persons were superior to non-creative persons in their verbal facility, fluency, flexibility and originality. Creative persons were considered more withdrawn and quiescent than non-creative persons. Individuality and non-conformity appeared to be desirable for creativity.

Taylor[6] concluded from his studies that creative persons are more devoted to autonomy, more self-sufficient, more independent in judgment, more open to the irrational in themselves, more stable,

[3] Jacob W. Getzels and Philip W. Jackson, *Creativity and Intelligence: Explorations with Gifted Students* (New York: John Wiley and Sons, Inc., 1962), p. 117.

[4] Harold Rugg, *Imagination: An Inquiry into the Sources and Conditions that Stimulate Creativity* (New York: Harper and Row, 1963), p. 54.

[5] J. E. Drevdahl, "Factors of Importance for Creativity," *Journal of Clinical Psychology*, XII (1956), pp. 21–26.

[6] C. W. Taylor, "Finding the Creative," *Scientific Research*, XXVIII (December 1961), pp. 6–11.

low in sociability, more interested in unconventional careers, more feminine in interests and characteristics, especially in awareness of one's impulses, more dominant and self-assertive, more complex as persons, more self-accepting, more resourceful and adventurous, more radical, more controlling of their own behavior by self-concept, and possibly more emotionally sensitive, and introverted but bold.

Torrance[7] found that the highly creative child is often psychologically estranged from his peers and his teacher. Creative children are accused of having wild and silly ideas. Many times their work is off the beaten track. They are able to summon up a great deal of humor and playfulness. These children tend to work in isolation. They are often uncooperative, and at times greedy and ego-centered.

Torrance does not attempt to say whether these behavior patterns *result* from the social pressures inflicted by the teacher or whether they are the *cause* of social estrangement. He does point out that it is the job of the school to help the highly creative child become less obnoxious without sacrificing his creativity.

At the Foundation for Human Research at Ann Arbor[8] studies set up to analyze creativity and conformity. have led to some interesting observations about creative personalities. Original people tend to have more energy and effectiveness; they are more impulsive and responsive to emotions than the unoriginal, they are more flexible. These researchers also found there were different kinds of conformity and that creative people tend to conform less than noncreative people even under group pressure. They are more willing, in other words, to support their own beliefs until proven to be wrong.

In a study of the personality and creativity of artists and writers, Drevdahl and Cattell[9] found that they differed from the normal population in being more intelligent, emotionally mature (ego strength), dominant, adventurous, emotionally sensitive, bohe-

[7] E. P. Torrance, "Current Research on the Nature of Creative Talent," *Journal of Counseling Psychology*, VI, No. 4 (1959), pp. 309–16.

[8] Foundation for Research on Human Behavior, *Creativity and Conformity*, ed. Carol Lundington (Ann Arbor, Michigan: Edwards Brothers, Inc., 1958).

[9] J. E. Drevdahl and R. B. Cattell, "Personality and Creativity in Artists and Writers," *Journal of Clinical Psychology*, XIV (April 1958), pp. 107–11.

mian, radical, self-sufficient, and of a high tension level. They were less subject to group standards and controls.

The creative person is most highly characterized by a relative absence of repression and suppression as mechanisms for the control of impulse and imagery. A creative person, because he expresses more than he suppresses has fuller access to his own life experiences, both conscious and unconscious. He has an openness to experience which allows him to take in more than the average person. He may appear, for example, to have more feminine interests because of this openness—because he does not deny expression to feminine interests and traits. This openness to experience makes it possible for him to speak openly about his life.[10]

The studies at Berkeley show that creative people have often had many psychological problems. They reveal that personal soundness is not an absence of problems but a way of reacting to them.

A creative person tends to prefer perceiving to judging. He is more interested and curious than the average person, more open and receptive. He reacts to experiences more fully in thought and feeling, although some, such as the artist, react more with feeling, while others, such as the scientist, react more with thought.

A creative person becomes to a high degree the individual he is capable of becoming—is more likely to fulfill his life potential. Sometimes he is judged to be socially irresponsible but this is perhaps because inward securities do not make it necessary for him to seek approval from others by following all the conventions of society. In reality, he may be very responsible yet not a conformist. Creative people are not deliberately non-conformists—but they are genuinely independent.

Creative people are inclined to be less interested in small details and facts as such and more concerned with their meanings and implications. Their philosophical values turn to the theoretical and esthetic. They seek not only truth but beauty as well.

The creative person delights in complex situations which demand he discover unifying principles to organize and integrate. He is often challenged by disorder.

[10] F. Barron, "The Disposition Towards Originality," *Journal of Abnormal and Social Psychology*, XLI (1955), pp. 478–85.

Creative power may reduce with age—but it is not age itself which causes this reduction; the factors that accompany age change do it.

In the personality development of the highly creative child three characteristics stand out. First, there is a tendency for him to gain a reputation for having wild and silly ideas. Second, his work is characterized by high productivity of ideas "off the beaten track." Third, his work is characterized by humor or playfulness. The three characteristics which emerge here would appear to be of considerable importance to the teacher and counselor in assisting the highly creative child to adjust without sacrificing his creativity.[11]

MacKinnon, in summarizing research, lists the following traits of creative people:

1. Creative people do not represent stereotypes.
2. Creative people are well above average in intelligence.
3. Creative people possess verbal intelligence, spatial intelligence, or sometimes both.
4. Creative persons have unusual capacity to record and retain and have readily available the experience of their life history.
5. They are discerning and observant in a different fashion; they are alert, capable of concentrating readily and shifting if appropriate; they are fluent in scanning thoughts and producing those that serve to solve the problems they undertake; they have a wide range of information at their command.
6. Intelligence alone will not tend to produce creativity. Creativity is the relevant absence of repression and suppression as mechanisms for the control of impulse and imagery. Repression operates against creativity, regardless of how intelligent a person may be.
7. The creative person, given to expression rather than suppression or repression, thus has fuller access to his own experience, both conscious and unconscious.
8. Openness to experience is one of the most striking characteristics of a highly creative person.
9. A highly creative person has a closer identification of feminine traits or characteristics in himself than non-creative. He is more open to feelings and emotions.
10. Everyone perceives and judges, but the creative person tends to prefer perceiving to judging. "Where a judging person

[11] E. P. Torrance, F. B. Baker and J. E. Bowers, *Explorations in Creative Thinking in the Early School Years* (Minneapolis: Bureau of Educational Research, University of Minnesota, 1959).

emphasizes the control and regulation of experience, the perceptive creative person is inclined to be more interested and curious, more open and receptive, seeking to experience life to the full."

11. Artists in general show a preference for feeling, scientists and engineers a preference for thinking. The architects are somewhere between the two groups.

12. A highly creative person is genuinely independent.

13. The creative person is relatively less interested in small detail, more concerned with meaning and implication. He is relatively uninterested in policing his own impulses and images or those of others.

14. He has preference for complexity and his delight is in the challenging and the unfinished.[12]

From the material previously quoted we might add these characteristics to MacKinnon's list:

15. Creative persons almost always display a good sense of humor.

16. Creative people tend to be more self-sufficient, more self-assertive, more self-accepting, more introverted but bold and more resourceful and self-accepting than the average person.

Torrance also made a summary of the studies which tried to identify the personality traits of a highly creative person. His list included, in addition to those already mentioned, the following traits:

1. strong affection
2. altruistic
3. always baffled by something
4. attracted to mysterious
5. attempts difficult jobs (sometimes too difficult)
6. bashful outwardly
7. constructive in criticism
8. courageous
9. deep and conscientious convictions
10. defies conventions of courtesy
11. defies conventions of health
12. desires to excel
13. determination
14. differentiated value-hierarchy
15. discontented
16. dominant (not in power sense)
17. a fault-finder

[12] Donald W. MacKinnon, "What Makes a Person Creative?" *Saturday Review* (February 1962), pp. 15–17+.

18. doesn't fear being thought "different"
19. feels whole parade is out of step
20. likes solitude
21. industrious
22. introversive
23. keeps unusual hours
24. lacks business ability
25. makes mistakes
26. never bored
27. not hostile or negativistic
28. oddities of habit
29. persistent
30. receptive to ideas of others
31. regresses occasionally
32. reserved
33. resolute
34. self-starter
35. sense of destiny
36. shuns power
37. sincere
38. not interested in small details
39. speculative
40. spirited in disagreement
41. tenacious
42. thorough
43. somewhat uncultured, primitive
44. unsophisticated, naive
45. unwilling to attempt anything on mere say so
46. visionary
47. versatile
48. willing to take risks[13]

Torrance feels that we may expect decreases in creative thinking ability and in creative production at about ages five, nine and twelve—and that these are all transitional periods in educational careers in our society.[14]

Dr. Torrance has also been interested in the effect of grouping on creativity.[15] He concludes that we may expect greater disruptive social stress when we divide classroom groups heterogeneously than

[13] E. P. Torrance, *Guiding Creative Talent* (Englewood Cliffs, N. J.: Prentice-Hall, Inc., 1962), pp. 66–67.

[14] E. P. Torrance, F. B. Baker and J. E. Bowers, *Explorations in Creative Thinking in the Early School Years* (Minneapolis: Bureau of Educational Research, University of Minnesota, 1954).

[15] E. P. Torrance, "Can Grouping Control Social Stress in Creative Abilities?" *Elementary School Journal*, LXII (December 1961), pp. 139–45.

when we divide them homogeneously. Creative thinking is likely to be stimulated by increasing social stress. When stress mounts beyond a certain point, however, thinking is disrupted and productivity diminishes. In general, therefore, heterogeneous grouping is more conducive to creativity than is homogeneous grouping.

The search for creative talent may be focused to a degree away from the individual and on the group of which he is a part. Clues for identifying creative people may be obtained by watching the reactions of other people. A creative person often causes tensions within a group because he presents a threat to the plans of the group. Striving for autonomy and solutions, he attempts to work his way around blocks to creativity erected by others and to overcome restrictions and organizational controls.

Gretzels and Jackson[16] explored the home environments and types of parents from which a high creative and a high intelligence group came. It was clear that the two groups of parents differed in their basic orientations toward themselves and their children. They differed in their childhood experiences, in the kind of education they had obtained, in the career lines they chose, and in the intellectual environment they provided in their home. They also differed in their attitudes toward their children, toward the education of their children, and toward the qualities they wanted their children to have. This would indicate that basic differences between highly creative and highly intelligent children have their beginnings in the home and family environment before they come to school. The high I.Q. family is one in which individual divergence is limited and risks minimized while the high creative family is one where individual divergence is admitted and risks are accepted.

They concluded from their research that the teacher tends to want the gifted child, as she defines him, in the classroom. The parents see other qualities as being more important than those used to define giftedness.[17]

They also found that there was *no* relationship between those qualities which the teachers defined in the gifted child (good marks, I.Q., and creativity) and the qualities which the teacher felt would make for success in adult life (getting along with others, goal directedness, and emotional stability). Parents ranked: (1) crea-

---

[16] Getzels and Jackson, *op. cit.*, p. 74.

[17] *Ibid.*, p. 118.

tivity (2) I.Q. and (3) goal directedness highest in defining the gifted child and (1) getting along with others (2) goal directedness and (3) emotional adjustment highest as making for success in life.

It is noteworthy that neither intelligence nor creativity, which had been ranked first respectively by teachers and parents as defining the gifted child, is included by either teachers or parents within the first three qualities making for adult success.[18]

These researchers also found that high I.Q. children and high creative children agreed on those qualities which make for success in adulthood and on the qualities teachers preferred in their students but they disagreed greatly on the qualities which they wanted for themselves.

The high I.Q. students rated the qualities they valued for themselves and those they believed to lead to success as quite close. The high creativity students showed almost no correlation in rating the qualities they valued for themselves and those they believed to lead to success.[19]

High I.Q. students showed a close relationship between the qualities they would like for themselves and the qualities they believed teachers like in students, suggesting that high I.Q. students may be highly teacher-oriented. On the other hand for the highly creative students the comparison showed little or no relationship, suggesting that this group is not highly teacher-oriented.

We have seen through Abraham Maslow's explanation of the hierarchy of needs how the socialization process can kill creativity (see page 35). Maslow also expounds the theory that every human being has "defense" and "growth" motivations within him. On the one hand he clings to safety and defensiveness out of fear, tending to regress, hanging on to the past, afraid to take chances, afraid of independence, freedom, separation. On the other hand he strives toward wholeness of self and uniqueness of self, toward full functioning of all his capacities, toward confidence in the face of the external world at the same time that he can accept his deepest, real unconscious self. This basic conflict between the defensive forces and the growth trends is imbedded in the human being, now and forever into the future.

[18] *Ibid.*, p. 119.
[19] *Ibid.*, pp. 35–36.

Therefore Maslow feels we can consider the process of healthy growth to be a never-ending series of free choice situations, confronting each individual at every point throughout his life, in which he must choose between the delights of safety and growth, dependence and independence. Safety has both anxieties and delights; growth has both anxieties and delights.[20] It appears according to the studies of Getzels and Jackson that high I.Q. students tend to favor the anxieties and delights of "safety" while high creatives tend to favor the anxieties and delights of "growth."

SUMMARY

From the research reported in this chapter there are some obvious contradictions about the social-emotional nature of the creative child. But, through it all, there run certain threads of consistency which help us to understand the creative child.

Viewed from the standpoint that most children succumb to the pressures of the socialization process, whereas creative children tend to remain individualistic, we may conclude that creative children are emotionally strong. Because of their unusual ideas and their willingness to stick to these ideas until they are disproven, they may alienate themselves from their peers. Often they must choose between social acceptance and their own personal intellectual challenge. When they choose intellectual challenge they may alienate friends, or, driven by enthusiasm and passion to follow through on an idea, they may appear to be different or not well-rounded.

Creative children like to attempt challenging, difficult and dangerous tasks; they strive to bring order out of disorder, sense out of chaos; they seek for a purpose. Because of their willingness to cope with the unsolved and the unusual, they may become psychologically estranged from other children. Because the problems they attack differ from purely "intellectual" problems, their behavior is different, they demonstrate characteristics different from accepted norms and their problems of adjustment are more difficult.

[20] A. H. Maslow, "Defense and Growth," *Merrill-Palmer Quarterly*, III (1956), pp. 31–38.

Creative children, therefore, may exhibit some types of behavior not readily accepted by the traditional teacher: low sociability; feminine interests; domination and self-assertion; introversion; boldness; silly ideas; playfulness; ego-centeredness; lack of cooperation; a certain amount of Bohemianism; radical outlooks; less interest in small details; non-conformity; lack of courtesy or adherence to conventions; emotionalism; self-satisfaction; excessive questioning; stubbornness; caprice; timidity; withdrawnness; and resistance to teacher domination.

It is difficult to determine at this point whether the less-acceptable personality factors in the creative child *result* from social pressures created by his teachers, parents and peers because they do not understand his social-emotional nature or whether these factors *cause* the social-emotional problems he encounters in his daily living.

Creative children do, however, also exhibit behavior which we would like to see more often in all citizens of a free society: high motivation; enthusiasm; sensitivity to and ability to define problems; fluency of ideas; flexibility of thinking; a drive to bring order from disorder; the ability to abstract and analyze; the willingness to stick to a goal or belief until disproven, even though peer disapproval is present; the ability to redefine and rearrange; the ability to evaluate and to synthesize; keen intuition and retention ability; verbal flexibility; a strong sense of humor; self-sufficiency; independence; interest in the less conventional; resourcefulness; a sense of adventure; self-acceptance; intelligence; achievement; great displays of energy; more emotional maturity; a capacity to deal with emotional or social problems; higher reaction to experience in terms of feeling and thought; verbal and spatial intelligence; openness to experience; willingness to tackle difficult jobs; courage; deep and conscientious convictions; determination and drive to excel; initiative; industriousness; persistence; receptivity to ideas of others; self-awareness; sensitivity to beauty; sincerity; versatility.

Now that common qualities and traits of creative children have been identified, much of the folklore surrounding creative people may be dispelled. Behavior often considered to be negative or unacceptable in the classroom may be interpreted as being acceptable, and even perhaps necessary, for creative growth. It would appear that one of the jobs of elementary school personnel is to take a fresh look at the behavior of children and to seek new interpretations of it. If the less accepted factors of personality in the creative child result from classroom organization and structure, new patterns of organization may be necessary so that creative children stand a strong chance of developing and are not plowed under—victims of their conforming teacher and their conforming peers—seeking status in the cocoon of society, rather than to develop their own particular contribution to society.

To the College Student

Can you be objective enough to ask yourself how the socialization process of college life has affected you? Are you an individual who contributes to class, and expresses himself well, or have you become a hopeless conformist to peer pressures? Or are you somewhere in between? Make a list of all the ways you feel you have remained an individual. Then make a list of the ways you feel you must conform. Which list is more heavily weighted?

Following are a group of quotations the author has overheard time and time again among his college students. Discuss each in terms of conformity versus individuality. Do you feel these quotes, lifted from context, are fair? Do they indicate the trend of thinking on our college campuses or are they exceptions?

- "I felt very strongly about that topic but I didn't say anything. After all, what's the use?"
- "I didn't agree with him at all but I'm not going to shoot off my big mouth and get him down on me. After all, I've got to pass this course."
- "Well, I went to Europe last summer and I know about that, but I wasn't going to sound off and make it look like I was bragging."
- "Do you think I'd do that and have him think I was apple-polishing?"
- "I really got a lot out of that course but I didn't tell him— I didn't want him to think I was a kook or something."
- "I really can't afford a new dress to the Prom so I guess I won't go—I've already worn my formal twice."

- "I'm not the only one who feels this way—all the kids in our class feel the same."

- "I really wanted to stay home and study for my test but the whole gang was going out for a coke and I couldn't be a wet blanket."

- "There was so much noise on my floor during study time, I just couldn't get to work."

Make a list of the characteristics you have which have been identified as those possessed by creative people.

Make a list of all the ways you can think of that you can be more individual in college.

Modern hair styles, manner of dress, and modern make-up are often used simply because they're in style. Assuming that the purpose of all of this is to make each individual more attractive, how do you feel many college students succeed? In conforming to style, people often neglect to take into consideration their own physical assets and deficiencies, and the adapted style sometimes accents the wrong features. Can you recall people who looked unattractive and lacked individuality although they wore nice clothes and used the latest hair styles and make-up? What are the basic elements necessary to consider in developing individuality in appearance?

After reading this book up to this point can you explain the current popularity of some film stars, singing stars, and television stars? What makes them stand out? Play some records of popular soloists in class and see how many the group can identify. Why is this possible?

In the musical, *Gypsy*, there is a song, "You've Gotta Have a Gimmick." A gimmick often identifies a program, a place or a person. Think of some "gimmicks" such as a theme song for a certain program. Is using a gimmick the same as creativity?

To the Classroom Teacher

Observe the children in your classroom who "bug" you. Then compare their qualities and characteristics with some of those listed in this chapter. Is it possible that some of them are exhibiting creative qualities?

The next time one of your pupils offers a "silly" idea to the class, ask him to explain it or develop it further. See what happens.

Review your daily program and ask yourself how many times during the day you organize your work so you can develop individuality in each child. Then note the times each child is expected to conform. Does one list far outbalance the other?

Look carefully at the organizational plan used in your school and ask yourself if it provides time for the development of creativity in each child? If not, could you effect any changes?

Note the list of Torrance on page 72–73 and check your daily program against it. How much time is spent each day in a deliberate effort to develop these creative qualities in children?

To the College Student and
the Classroom Teacher

Construct an evaluation check sheet on those qualities which tend to be apparent in creative children. Use the list suggested in the summary of this chapter. Ditto your list and check one off for each child in the classroom using a 1–5 scale. Before you do this, make a list of the ten children you feel are most creative in the class. Then check the sheets and pull out the ten who score highest on the individual qualities. Compare your original lists with the ten check sheets. How good are you at predicting creativity in boys and girls?

Make a list of activities such as folk dancing, which would not create a stigma regarding sex roles but which would allow boys and girls in your classroom to participate in the roles of the opposite sex.

Select a favorite author, movie star, poet or any great creative person you have admired. Do some research on his life. Which of the qualities mentioned in this chapter did this highly creative person possess?

SELECTED BIBLIOGRAPHY

Bloom, B. S. "Some Effects of Cultural, Social and Educational Conditions on Creativity" in *The Second University of Utah Conference on the Identification of Creative Scientific Talent*. Salt Lake City: University of Utah Press, 1958.

Carlson, Ruth K. "Emergence of Creative Personality," *Childhood Education*, XXXVI (1960), 402–04.

Hammer, E. F. "Emotional Stability and Creativity," *Percept. Mot. Skills*, XII (1961), 102.

Lasswell, H. D. "The Social Setting of Creativity" in H. Anderson (ed.). *Creativity and Its Cultivation*. New York: Harper and Brothers, 1959.

Lehner, George and Kube, F. J. and Ella. *The Dynamics of Personal Adjustment*. Englewood Cliffs, N. J.: Prentice-Hall, Inc., 1955.

Meer, B. and Stern, M. L. "Measures of Intelligence and Creativity," in *Creativity and the Individual*. Glencoe, Illinois: The Free Press, 1960.

Stein, Morris I. and Heinze, Shirley. *Creativity and the Individual*. Glencoe, Illinois: The Free Press, 1960.

Torrance, E. Paul. *Guiding Creative Talent*. Englewood Cliffs, N. J.: Prentice-Hall, Inc., 1962.

*T*o construct and to create are quite different. A thing
constructed can only be loved after it is constructed,
but a thing created is loved before it exists.[1]

—————————————————Gilbert Keith Chesterton

[1] Source unknown.

VI——The Process
of Creativity

CREATIVITY is a process and a product. Creativity, in our current life, is most easily measured or identified by the product. It is not always possible to evaluate a product as a creative one for that which often adpears to be creative may in actuality be a copy or an imitation.

THE PRODUCT

To understand that which constitutes the creative product at the individual level, we may refer to our earlier definition of creativity. A creative product is something new to the child which comes about as a result of the reassembling of selected experiences from his past.

Marksberry[2] classifies creativity into three types on the basis of the object produced: under the first type, unique communication, she includes creative writing and art experiences; under the second type she includes problem-solving, critical thinking, comprehension, application, analysis, and evaluation; under

[2] Mary Lee Marksberry, *Foundation of Creativity* (New York: Harper and Row, 1963), p. 37.

the third type she includes the formation of appropriate hypotheses in light of known facts and the ability to modify such hypotheses when new factors and considerations are found, the ability to make social studies generalizations, word-attack generalizations, mathematical discoveries, and science generalizations.

Marksberry's classifications indicate that creative products may result through the conscious use of most areas of the school curriculum if teachers will accept the fact that products include the total list above.

THE PROCESS

The process of creativity is at least as important as the product. Research in the past ten years has been directed toward identifying the process of creativity. Once the process is understood, teachers will be better able to recognize creative behavior and will be better able to understand how to set conditions to develop creativity.

Most writers agree that the creative act is a highly organized system of response to some stimuli. They also agree that certain phases are apparent in this process but there is some disagreement over just exactly what those phases are. They also agree that some creativity seems to be spontaneous.

Understanding of the creative process up to this time leads us to believe that there may be more than one method of creating; that different problems call for different methods. Research has not been conclusive as yet, and many of the guidelines must be taken from the theorists and the students in this area. Dr. Edmund Sinnott[3] believes that two major methods appear to be operative in the process. One is primarily deductive and the other spontaneous. The deductive method involves a direct frontal assault on a problem—gathering facts and ideas together and deliberately seeking for new relationships between them. The deductive method is used by scientists in establishing new theories. The spontaneous method is defined as a sudden flash of insight which causes a new idea to arise, seemingly out of nothing. Dr. Sinnott feels that this happens only when an individual has been immersed in a problem

[3] E. Sinnott, "The Creativeness of Life," in *Creativity and Its Cultivation*, ed. Harold H. Anderson (New York: Harper and Brothers, 1959), Chapter 2.

and has been coping with the half-formed products in his imagination over a period of time. Often, after mulling over this problem for days, the creative impulse seems to come spontaneously.

At one of three conferences on *Creativity as a Process* sponsored by the Institute of Contemporary Art during 1956–58[4] the participants explored six themes or phases that can be observed whenever creativity is at work: (1) involvement-detachment (the process of relating personally to the problem and then being able to draw back and see it as a problem); (2) speculation (the ability to advance from the actual experience to a tentative one); (3) deferment (the willingness to wait for a shadowy, but more rewarding future and give up immediate glittering success); (4) autonomy (the point where the creative product begins to have a personality of its own and begins to tell the creator what to do); (5) purposiveness (the drive which finally comes to create the object just for the sake of creating it); and (6) use of the commonplace (the place from which beginnings are made because there is no wish to return to this mediocre state).

In her book, *Foundation of Creativity*, Mary Lee Marksberry draws together the various theories of the creative process into a very acceptable one.

She feels that there is enough evidence to conclude that the creative process consists of four definite stages and that they are: (1) a period of preparation, (2) a period of incubation, (3) a period of insight, illumination or inspiration and (4) a period of verification, elaboration, perfecting and evaluation. She feels creativeness can be developed in the elementary school by keeping these steps in mind and she gives illustrations to show how creativeness can be developed in writing, in art, in problem-solving and in deriving sets of abstract relations.

In Marksberry's classification, the long-range period of preparation encompasses all the life experiences upon which a child draws for any particular creative act. The immediate preparation begins when a child has a desire strong enough to trigger activity. It can vary in length depending on the individual, the nature of the problem and the knowledge, skills and habits of the individual. If insight does not come as a gradual illumination gained through

[4] William J. J. Gordon, *Conference on Creativity as a Process*, Oct. 10–12, 1956. Arden House, Harriman, N. Y. (Institute on Contemporary Art.)

these activities little progress appears to be made in solving the problem.

The period of incubation is that time of activity when the individual weighs the problem and searches for a solution. This is often a very frustrating, restless period and often is accompanied by feelings of inferiority.

Marksberry defines the period of insight as that when either by a flash or a hunch the creator sees the answer. These moments are marked by feelings of success and accomplishment.

The period of verification is the concluding part of the process and includes elaboration, perfecting and evaluation. It is during this period that the creator checks, tests, criticizes and polishes the solution until he is satisfied with it.[5]

In his book, *Imagination: An Inquiry Into the Sources and Conditions that Stimulate Creativity* Rugg defines four stages of the creative process: first, a preparatory conscious period of baffled struggle; second, an interlude in which the worker apparently gives up, pushes the problem back or down or "out of mind"—more properly into another compartment of "mind"—leaving it for the unconscious to work upon; third, a sudden and unexpected "flash of insight," coming with such certitude that a logical statement of it can be immediately prepared; fourth, a period of verification, critical testing, and reconstruction.[6]

Rugg's and Marksberry's explanations of the creative process seem to have much in common.

It would seem that other elements besides intellect enter into creative processes. Sprecher,[7] for instance, in a survey of descriptions of creative people among engineers, found that not only were ideas considered important in creative production but so were work habits. Being independent, planning work activities, following through on projects, developing comprehensive and thorough answers—these characteristics were considered as important to creativity as the production of unusual ideas or practical valuable ideas.

[5] Marksberry, *op. cit.*, pp. 17–20.

[6] Harold Rugg, *Imagination: An Inquiry into the Sources and Conditions that Stimulate Creativity* (New York: Harper and Row, 1963), p. 6.

[7] Thomas B. Sprecher, "A Proposal for Identifying the Meaning of Creativity" in *Scientific Creativity: Its Recognition and Development* by Calvin W. Taylor and Frank Barron (eds.) (New York: John Wiley and Sons, 1963), pp. 87–88.

Marksberry recognizes two types of skills or abilities used in creative production—psychomotor skills and intellectual abilities. Under psychomotor skills she includes apprehending and manipulating objects in the environment, constructing symbols, and using the body for expressing ideas or feelings. Under intellectual skills she includes critical thinking, reflective thinking and problem-solving.[8]

Guilford,[9] in response to Wallas'[10] classification of the creative process into four phases—preparation, incubation, illumination, and revision—maintained that these phases were superficial. He feels that motivational factors (interests and attitudes) as well as temperament must make a significant contribution. He points out that a full account of creative-artistic performances involves abilities that are not primarily creative. He further states that thinking factors fall into three general groups, based upon the kind of *action* performed. There is a group of *cognition* factors, a group of *production* factors and a group of *evaluation* factors. We become aware of the things with which we are confronted and we produce something of our own in response to that awareness, and we evaluate our products of thought. A total creative act involves all three aspects—cognition, production and evaluation.

In productive thinking a logical distinction appears—the thinking which converges on one right answer—convergent thinking, and the thinking which produces many novel, different answers—divergent thinking. In divergent thinking we find the most obvious indication of creativity.

More recent research in the field has shown Guilford's concepts to be true to a great degree.

CREATIVITY IS DEVELOPMENTAL

To understand the creative process completely, we must not overlook earlier studies in the area of child development. Much of the work of Lowenfeld, Gesell, Alschuler and others would indicate

[8] Marksberry, *op. cit.*, p. 15.

[9] J. P. Guilford, "Creative Abilities in the Arts," *Psychological Review*, LXIV (1957), pp. 110–18.

[10] Graham Wallas, *The Art of Thought* (New York: Harcourt, 1926).

that the creative process depends to some degree on the age and experiential background of the child.

Lowenfeld identified various stages through which a child develops his ability to create with paint. These particular stages indicate a long-range development rather than a short-range process. Alschuler and Hartwick[11] found evidence that there is a strong relationship between the emotional structure of the child and his choice of paints, choice of strokes, technique of working, etc. It seems safe to say that the age of the child and his social-emotional structure may be a strong influence on the creative processes he employs.

Our understandings of creative processes may be broadened by applying what we know about social growth, concept formation, value formation, physical change in body structure and other knowledge about child growth and development to Marksberry's basic guides to recognizing the creative process.

SUMMARY

Marksberry summarizes the work of many researchers by saying the creative process is a series of experiences or part processes, each of which continues what has gone on in preceding experiences and leads directly into other experiences until the final whole is realized. Each experience is a problem-solving situation making its contribution to the overall problem. Thus, we can divide the creative process into four separate stages: a period of preparation; a period of incubation; a period of insight, illumination, or inspiration; and a period of verification, elaboration, perfecting and evaluation.[12]

To the College Student

Observe a child or a roommate in the process of creating. This may be a short-range or a long-range observation. Can you identify any of Marksberry's four steps in the process of creativity?

[11] Rose H. Alschuler and La Berta W. Hattwick, *Painting and Personality: A Study of Young Children* (Chicago: University of Chicago Press, 1947).

[12] Marksberry, *op. cit.*, p. 17.

Suppose you were given the job of designing a better desk lamp. Under what specific heads would you break down this general problem?

Identify five areas of our culture that need close scrutiny because they pose serious problems. Divide the class into five groups with each group assigned a problem to discuss. Have each group tackle the problem while one person appointed as observer takes notes on group behavior. Later, compare notes and try to identify the stages of creative thinking that took place.

Which of the following assignments given to a sixth grade class are most likely to develop creativity in the children? Discuss why.

- "Write a poem about spring for English class tomorrow."

- "Look around you for the next two weeks and at that time, hand in a paper with a list of inventions you would like to have someone make and explain why."

- "You will have four themes to write this semester. They may be on any topic, in any form, and handed in at any time. As soon as you decide what you are going to do I should like a note from you on a 3 x 5 card stating your topics."

- "Take out your paper and pencils and write a theme for me about how you spent your summer vacation."

To the Classroom Teacher

Think of the assignments you have given children over the last three days. How many of them really allowed the children to develop through the total creative process? How could you change these assignments so they might allow children to really develop creatively?

Discuss the following statements with other teachers:

- The most important role played by the teacher in the creative process is Step I: The period of preparation. This implies the teacher is responsible for introducing the child to the problem.

- The creative process never occurs spontaneously.

- If I teach one or two lessons a day geared to developing creativity, I shall substantially raise the creative thinking powers of my students.

- It is possible to accumulate too many facts before starting to solve a problem.

Think of all the reasons why children might be attracted to a problem and become involved in finding a creative solution to it. Take a sample problem if you have trouble.

To the College Student and
the Classroom Teacher

Make a list of principles that should underlie an assignment if it is to permit the functioning of the creative process.

Inasmuch as the first step in the creative process is the period of preparation and involvement, examine the following statements culled from the speech of teachers and react to them. Which ones make you want to be involved and which do not?

- "Open your workbooks to page 36."
- "In this box I have something and if I open it we will have a problem to solve."
- "Read the first two paragraphs to find the answer to the questions on the board."
- "I have a magic ring in my pocket."
- "We have broken a school rule because there was a fight on the playground. We will have to decide what to do about it. In order to fully understand what happened so we can make our decision wisely I am going to ask John and Peter to show us what happened by using the puppets."

From the above quotations can you believe that just by the way they talk teachers can motivate children to creative problem-solving?

List the advantages of a teacher and student teacher teaming up on a creative project with the children in your classroom.

Why is individual thinking still important in creative production?

How many creative ideas can you come up with for solving the following two problems: How can we convince the teachers of our school of the value of creative teaching and what can we do to implement it?

Selected Bibliography

Anderson, Harold H. *Creativity and Its Cultivation.* New York: Harper and Brothers, 1959.

Bergson, Henry Louis. *The Creative Mind.* New York: Philosophical Library, 1946.

Follett, M. D. *Creative Experience.* New York: Longmans Green, 1954.

Ghiselin, B. *The Creative Process.* New York: Mentor Books, 1955.

Givens, P. R. "Identifying and Encouraging Creative Processes," *Journal of Higher Education,* XXXIII (1962), 295–301.

Kubie, L. S. *Neurotic Distortion of the Creative Process.* University of Kansas Press, 1958.

Maltzman, I. *et al.* "Experimental Studies in the Training of Originality," *Psychological Monographs, General and Applied.* Los Angeles, University of California, LXXIV, No. 6 (1960), 11–17.

Marksberry, Mary Lee. *Foundation of Creativity.* New York: Harper and Row, 1963.

Murphy, Gardner. *Human Potentialities.* New York: Basic Books, Inc., 1958.

Patrick, Catherine. *What is Creative Thinking?* New York: Philosophical Library, 1955.

Smith, Paul (ed.). *An Examination of the Creative Process.* New York: Publishers Inc., 1959.

Stein, M. I. and Heine, S. *Creativity and the Individual.* Glencoe, Ill.: The Free Press, 1960.

Taylor, Calvin (ed.). *The Third Research Conference on the Identification of Creative Scientific Talent.* Salt Lake City: University of Utah Press, 1959.

Wertheimer, M. *Productive Thinking.* (rev. ed.) New York: Harper and Brothers, 1959.

CREATIVITY
CAN BE DEVELOPED
AND EXPRESSED
IN
MANY WAYS . . .

. . . by preparing food . . .

. . . building a rocket ship with blocks . . .

. . . by producing television shows . . .

. . . using words and blocks to tell about a circus . . .

. . . making marionettes . . .

. . . presenting puppet plays . . .

. . . dancing . . .

. . by painting murals . . .

. . . and by running a travel bureau.

*CREATIVITY
CAN BE DEVELOPED
AND EXPRESSED
IN
MANY WAYS . . .*

PART
TWO

THE NURTURE
OF
CREATIVITY

AN OVERVIEW

IT IS THE function of the scientist, the philosopher, and the psychologist to investigate the nature of man. It is the function of the educator to elicit knowledge from these investigations and to inject this knowledge into the life stream of the culture.

The following excerpt from "Clues to Creative Teaching," an article by Calvin Taylor, makes a serious contribution to our thinking along these lines:

We are all challenged with the problem of bridging the gap between research findings and educational practice. Today there is scanty assurance that what is known through research will quickly—or ever—be applied in the classroom, though there is a great and immediate need for doing so. The best illustration of this need is the area of creativity, where new and exciting research findings pose many novel changes to education.

But the teacher and the educational administrator may say, "The research stuff isn't manageable for our use." And they are right. "Educational engineers" are needed to help bridge the gap, but in general such specialists do not yet exist. The soundest approach at present is to admit that not much is known by anyone about the necessary bridging activities, and to set forth without delay to discover how to develop them ourselves. We must learn how to translate research findings so they become suitable and applicable, ready to be installed in classrooms.[1]

Dr. Taylor has stated well the major role of the educator in the immediate years ahead. One of the most challenging tasks facing all educators in the coming decade is to develop techniques by which creativity can be nurtured. The accumulating knowledge reported in the first part of this volume is pointing the direction to be taken.

Creative teaching is not new. There have always been creative teachers, some have become famous for their work: Hughes Mearns, Natalie Cole, Mauree Appelgate, Laura Zirbes and others. These people developed creativity in children by instinct more than any other way. Their writings are rich with examples of the creative products of children. These people could well be labeled the "educational engineers" about whom Dr. Taylor speaks.

There are others who have not been idle over these past years. For five years I have worked with teachers trying myself to translate this

[1] Calvin W. Taylor, "Clues to Creative Teaching," *The Instructor* (September, 1963) p. 5.

research into classroom methodology and trying to help other teachers see how it might be done. That we have had a satisfying amount of success can best be measured by what has happened to the children with whom we worked and the products they have produced. That is what the remainder of this series of books is about: ways to develop creativity in children through all areas of the curriculum through the application of basic principles reported by research.

In the second part of this volume, I report our interpretation of this research and give both general and specific illustrations of the application of these principles to classroom methodology.

*T**he peculiar mark of the creative teacher—as different from all other businesses of man—is not his learning alone but his ability to transform others by the contagion of his own peculiar creative powers. If he can only repeat the studied work of another but is unable out of all that to create something of his very own, his teaching will be of minor importance.*

Good teaching is not solely the business of instructing; it is also the art of influencing another. Primarily, it is the job of uncovering and enlarging native gifts of insight, feeling, and thinking . . .

No superior outcome is possible . . . without the creative teacher.[1]

—HUGHES MEARNS

---

[1] Hughes Mearns, *Creative Power: The Education of Youth in the Creative Arts* (Rev. ed.; New York: Dover Publications, Inc., 1958), p. 267 and p. 252.

VII——The Meaning
and Method
of Creative Teaching

CREATIVE teaching is a METHOD of teaching. It is based on a set of principles and theories which have emerged in recent years as a result of observation and research in the area of creativity. These principles are revolutionizing our concepts of method.

Although the way is not perfectly clear, we need wait no longer to put into practice the information which shows the way to creative teaching and the development of creativity in young people. While we are waiting for more evidence to be collected we can begin to design a new methodology, new at least to those teachers who have not been aware of the need for creative teaching. And we can provide the many creative teachers who already exist further support for their unique work.

THE PROBLEM OF METHOD

In the past, it was the custom in teacher training institutions to teach students *how* to teach. I remember well my first student teaching experience. I spent long hours writing detailed lesson plans before I appeared before a class. I have come to realize that every good teacher lays plans very carefully. But not plans like the ones I wrote then. They did not free me to teach—they shackled me so that I could not really teach. Actually I prepared a script from which I could perform. Here is an excerpt from one of the plans from which I taught during my first student teaching experience:

Lesson Plan
Making the Letter "A"
Grade 3

OBJECTIVE: To teach the proper formation of the cursive small and capital letter "A."

MATERIALS: 32 Sheets Primary paper
32 Pencils
Blackboard liner
Chalk
Pictures of an apple and an apple seed.

MOTIVATION: Ask first student in each row to pass out paper for his row.

Teacher: Good Morning. My name is Mr. Smith. This morning we are going to work together to learn something new. I have here a picture. What is it a picture of?

Student: It is an apple.

PROCEDURE

Teacher: Yes, it is an apple. If I were to cut the apple in half, what would I find in the middle?

Student: A seed.

Teacher: That is right—an apple seed. And here is a picture of the 2 seeds I would find in the middle of the apple. Can anyone tell me what is the name of the letter at the beginning of the word, "apple"?

Student: "A."

Teacher: That is correct. It is called an "A." Let us write the word apple on the blackboard and look at the first letter.

(Teacher writes the word "apple" on the chalkboard.)

Notice the first letter. It is an "A." Today we are going to learn how to make the letter "A" correctly.

(Teacher draws the first part of the capital "A" off to one side of the board like this *Ο* .)

Teacher: Now, what does this look like?

Student: An apple seed.

Teacher: Good! Yes, it looks like an apple seed. That is why it is so easy to remember how to make an "A." It is the letter that begins the word apple and it is shaped like the seed that is in the apple. Let us look at the big "A" first.

(Teacher draws lines on the board with a liner.)

Teacher: Now notice that the big "A" begins at the top line. We draw a big apple seed that touches the bottom line and then we put a tail on it, like this ____*Α*____ . Now let us see if you can make one. Assume writing positions. Let me see all feet flat on the floor, backs straight, papers on desk pointed to the center of your body.

(Teacher checks positions.)

That is good. Now, all hands on desk. Ready, one!

(Children raise hands above desk.)

Two!

(Children drop hands—left hand over top of paper to hold it in place, right hand picks up pencil and holds it over paper.)

Teacher: That is good. Let's see—are our wrists flat? Are our pencils pointing over our right shoulders? Then watch me as I draw another big "A." I will count for you like this: "One" and you will draw the seed ____*Ο*____ , then "Two," and you will pull your hand down to make the tail ____*Α*____ , like this. Let's watch one more—"One,–Two, One,–Two." Now you try—"One, Two, etc."

A cursory examination of this plan makes it appear ridiculous. How well I remember the day I taught it! I was told to appear in the village school at exactly 10:30 and there I would meet my supervisor outside the door of Miss Walker's third grade. So, at 10:25 I appeared. My supervisor also appeared and together we walked into Miss Walker's third grade where some 32 children sat in desks, which were arranged in long rows and nailed to the floor. The children, too, appeared to be nailed to the floor. Not once during the whole 45 minutes of my "lesson" did they move from their seats—they sat with hands folded, eyes fastened on me, responding to my every direction. I remember one of the points on which I was graded was how quiet I could keep my class. I must have received the coveted A in that respect. I don't recall that any child spoke without being called on during the whole time I performed. The greatest catastrophe of the entire lesson was when I asked Allen "What does this look like?" (as I drew a shape like this $\mathcal{O}$ on the board). He was, according to my carefully written and approved plan, supposed to say "an apple seed," and instead he said, "a fish." This nearly "threw" me but fortunately I had presence of mind enough to dispose of him, mentally at least, as an uncooperative and unimaginative child, probably mentally retarded, and immediately asked someone else who gave me my anticipated answer. So the lesson progressed. As silently as I came at 10:30, I left at 11:15. All the while my supervisor and Miss Walker sat in the back of the room, in opposite corners, taking notes and nodding encouragement. Those notes were later used in a conference back at the training school. I remember that the criticisms of my lesson were of this nature: Melvin had been very wiggly and I had not reprimanded him; I did keep good "control"; my plan was well worked out and I "anticipated" well; I had thought through my distribution of materials well, etc.

No comments were made about the fact that I hadn't planned for any individual differences in those children; no mention was made of evaluation—whether or not I had accomplished my goals; there was no concern about the fact that I had learned nothing from the children. It did not seem so absurd then that I did not know one single child by name but had a seating chart and could call on the wiggly ones by consulting it. The main concern was my performance—with emphasis on control and presentation. As I look back at this experience some 30 years after it happened I realize that *method* meant preplanned and premeditated performance.

We have come a long way since then in our understanding of real pedagogy. But, because method in those days meant the *one* way of presenting a lesson, the teaching profession is full of teachers who teach *one* way—or use *a* method. Our teacher training institutions of thirty to fifty years ago did a good job in training teachers the way they thought was correct. This is evidenced by the number of teachers who were taught so well that they still teach the same material in the same way today, regardless of new knowledge of children and the manner in which they learn, and new theories of pedagogy.

Thousands of young people left those institutions of a few years back with files full of "plans" to follow—and other sorts of patterns to copy. Regardless of the places they went to teach, regardless of the kinds of children they faced in their classrooms, the plans and patterns were dusted off and used. I remember one of my most cherished possessions was a file of folders labeled by the months of the year. In each folder there were stencils which I had laboriously traced in the library files and cut from chip board: squirrels, pumpkins, acorns, oak leaves, and maple leaves for October; turkeys, Pilgrims, vegetables, fruits, fireplaces and log cabins for November and so on. And year after year those patterns, along with my carefully written plans, were to be dragged out and used. That, at least, was the general theory: a nice, fat file contained all the ideas a teacher ever needed for a whole year. Then he had it made. Why go to summer school? Why worry about anything new? He had his plans—the result of his many years of experience—and he could leave school with the children and still be well prepared for the next day.

There were some new ideas appearing on the horizon. We were taught to teach reading by a "sight" method. Educators were arguing over the merits of putting geography and history into a larger body of material and calling it social studies. Some places in the country were already doing this by a startling new method called unit teaching.

But the masses of teachers being trained then were loyal to the plans and patterns of their training. Experience has taught some of them the limitations of such training for life in a technological age. Advanced training has taught many others how to be good teachers, and a combination of training and evaluated experiences has produced many excellent, creative teachers.

But many, unfortunately have not changed. And because, to this day, many of them have left such negative impressions on the adults and the youth of America, we tend to revolt against them by rebelling against the *METHODS* they use.

We attack method and pedagogy as though they were responsible for all educational ills. We suggest that teachers bound to METHOD become uncreative and sterile in their teaching. We suggest the abolition of METHOD even to the extent that we abolish methods courses in our colleges of education and substitute more content courses in Liberal Arts.

This is impossible as well as impractical. Every teacher must have a "way" to teach. To abolish method means only that we give up what may be a carefully planned technique and substitute no particular technique at all. In such a situation, no particular technique at all becomes the method of teaching. The use of *"no method"* is a *method*, often the poorest method that could be used.

The major problem confronting us is that in attempting to be scientific about teaching, teachers have often been trained instead to be unthinking and illogical about it. The dogmatic approach to methodology has caused many teachers to confuse real scientific research with the opinions of experts. The teaching of reading in today's schools is a good illustration: experts in the area have tended to "gang up" on the teachers with an impregnable wall of opinion which teachers often accept as science simply because all experts agree on it. While this may have value when no research is available it also tends to hinder imaginative research because few people dare to defy the opinions of the experts. As a result, no significant change in methodology in the teaching of reading has occurred in this country in thirty years until recently.

The major drawback of methodology can be simply stated: teachers in the past were taught to be slaves to a method or plan, rather than masters of it, and teaching was seen as an imitative process—one where a student was given a good "grade" when he performed in a manner quite like his master teacher. Minor changes were allowed, of course, but teaching was largely a mimetic act—perpetuated year after year with only minor changes and little variation. Just as teachers went into teaching with their file of chipboard patterns, they themselves were the products of the teaching of chipboard ideas. The teacher brought little to the teaching *act*. Her personality was the major contribution (as it still is) to her teaching and determined to a great degree whether or not she was a superior teacher.

In other words, teachers were not taught to be creative in their teaching. Just as individuality emerges in spite of suffocating influences in children, in some teachers it refused to be confined and spilled forth—and these people became the creative teachers of the past.

We knew little about creativity and how to develop creative teachers until recently. There is still much to be learned, but the emerging frontier of research is telling us some things which are important to consider in the training of teachers.

One of the most important of these is that teaching is *not* a mimetic process. Instead of mimicking to a minute degree that which a master teacher does, a creative teacher must establish patterns of her own. The "differentness" and "oddness" so often frowned on or accepted as justification for the success of a few daring teachers *is the very thing we are after in all teachers*. The thing that makes all teaching great is the degree to which every teacher can take basic principles of pedagogy and translate them into unusual, different, and original acts of teaching. Methodology, under this concept is not "fixed"—it varies continually. These teachers are the ones who "never teach the same thing twice in the same way" or "never teach the same thing to all the pupils in the same manner." Teaching is not mimetic under these circumstances, it is different, changing, dynamic, real—and teachers are not puppets; they bring to teaching the greatest gift they can bring—*themselves*—their ideas, their knowledge, their skill, their personalities, their differences. They become, because of this, self-actualized. They never get into the proverbial rut because each year is a new experience.

That is what creative teaching is—that is what research is telling us about the development of creativity. But creativity in children can only be developed when teacher training institutions spend a major portion of their time helping teachers to be creative themselves.

There is a powerful difference between my method of teaching the writing lesson above, and the way I taught creative writing in Jody's class and the lesson in the culturally deprived area. The power that makes the difference is the *creative method*.

Some Blocks to Creative Teaching

There are many blocks to creative teaching, all of which are related to methodology. Some of them can be eliminated by changing the emphasis in the teacher-training program. But many of them exist in the teaching field itself, and can only be removed by administrators who understand the process and value of creative teaching.

1. *Lack of Intelligence:* Lack of intelligence is one such block. There is a high correlation between real creativity and intelligence. Teacher training institutions must be selective and must strive to attract highly intelligent candidates to the teaching profession.

2. *Conformity:* Conformity is one of the greatest enemies of creativity. Methods courses in teacher training institutions need to help teachers-in-training determine when conformity is necessary to maintain cohesiveness in a group but should also encourage students to evolve their own application of the generally accepted principles of education. Minute details need not be spelled out (such as "this is the way we present the vowel sound 'a'"). The teacher's plan should be based on the general principles and knowledge she has learned: child psychology, her understanding of child growth and development, her knowledge of the learning process, her knowledge of scope and sequence of curriculum development, her knowledge of teaching resources and classroom organization, her understanding of the sociological, anthropological and philosophical nature of the situation, her knowledge of the creative process and her knowledge of any basic research in this specific area of instruction. Rather than "a" method being defined, limitless illustrations should be discussed as to how an idea might be put across or has been put across by creative teachers. Plans written for teaching should be valued for their uniqueness rather than their similarity.

3. *Overplanning:* My lesson in Miss Walker's third grade is a good example of overplanning. I knew exactly what I was going

to say and do every moment I was in that room! Careful plans are important—but not to the degree that the teacher can put words into the mouths of the children themselves, and refuse to accept any other words! Creativity is not a guessing game where children try to "guess" the answer or the response which the teacher wants. It is, to a great degree, unpredictable. If a teacher has in mind the *exact* answers children will give or the exact product they will make, creative teaching is not taking place. It has already been stated that creative teaching means taking each child to a certain level in the learning process and then letting him go it alone. The product is unpredictable. Planning such as I did for Miss Walker's children left no possible way for them to discover or invent. I allowed them to reach their goal only by following my prescribed plan, bit by bit. Goals must be clear in planning, and procedures must be clear also, but flexibility is necessary.

4. *Planning the Same for All Children:* There should be no such thing as "a" plan. Even within a master plan there must be a plan for every one of the children in a class. I made no allowances in my plan for the many patterns of learning present in that third grade. I gave no consideration to the individual abilities or the backlog of individual experiences. I was presumptuous enough to assume that all children could learn *my* way—all children were of *my* ability. Creativeness is an individual thing—and can best be developed in situations where individual contributions of children can be brought out and respected. Individualized teaching is in keeping with our basic democratic goals and necessary to develop the full potential of all children. It need not necessarily be done in small groups. This has been demonstrated in some of the illustrations given in Part I of this book.

5. *Closed Questions:* The "guessing game" questions I asked in Miss Walker's room are good examples of how real critical or creative thinking can be killed off. Perhaps this type of questioning is necessary occasionally but it should never be *the* predominant type of question used. Well planned questions develop convergent and divergent, critical and creative thinking processes among most of the children most of the time. They keep children thinking. They are often referred to as "open-ended" questions and are described more fully in the texts which supplement this book.

One teacher asks, "What is the population of Nevada?" and calls a child's name. The child who is called upon gropes around in his memory for the one figure he has read in his textbook. That is the only correct answer—it is a closed question. The rest of the children give a sigh of relief that they do not have to answer it and then daydream until the next question is asked or until the next name is called.

Another teacher has a child copy various population figures on the chalkboard. After the children study them she makes this observation: "Although the United States is growing in population so rapidly we almost cannot keep up with the figures, we will notice by these figures that not *all* states are growing. Note for instance that in 1961 Maine and Vermont lost people, while Nevada and Arizona (desert states) and California (a dry state) grew the fastest. Why?" This is a question which is open-ended: it suggests the gathering of evidence, the weighing of that evidence, promotes discussion, welcomes opinion, paves the way for decision and evaluation. This is open-ended learning leading to creative thinking. This is the type of question that can be used with *all* children because all can find material to help answer it. Knowledge for knowledge's sake is expanded to knowledge put to use.

6. *Abuse of Gimmicks:* Gimmicks have been used since time immemorial. Many great changes in education were brought about through the use of gimmicks; the *blocks* of Montessori, the *garden* of Froebel, the *materials* of Pestalozzi, the *object* lessons of Sheldon. Now more than ever our educational culture is full of them: flannel boards, flash cards, moving picture projectors, pocket charts, bulletin boards, field trips, television, teaching machines, dioramas, murals, workbooks—all can be classified as gimmicks.

There is nothing wrong with gimmicks. What is wrong is the uncreative way they have been used. When used uncreatively, gimmicks rarely fulfill the purpose for which they were intended. The creative use of a gimmick can result in some excellent teaching. We have already seen this in the use of the black light and the fluorescent chalk described on page 17. The teaching machine is a gimmick. Used properly, it can be of value. Teachers must be aware, however, that teaching machines, like all gimmicks, have their limitations. They are only aids—and only of value to the degree that they help accomplish those objectives the teacher is attempting to accomplish. At this writing it is difficult to see how teaching machines, as such, can contribute much to the development of creativity within the individual. Of necessity, they are constructed with the closed question and are concerned with the perpetuation of knowledge rather than with the more creative objectives of the school.

Audio-visual aids are gimmicks. If used properly they can be a boon to the development of creativity. When used solely as time-fillers, however, they can be a waste of time. Much can often be accomplished in ten minutes with a good audio-visual aid that would take the teacher an hour to accomplish with words. But in the phrase "audio-visual aids," the word "AIDS" needs to be capitalized. They can offer nothing to the development of creativity without the teacher. Hundreds of ways of using audio-visual aids to develop creativity are shown in the books which accompany this volume. In Volume IV a chapter is devoted to ways of developing creativity through the use of audio-visual aids.

7. *Overuse of the Textbook:* One of the reasons why creative teaching has been checked in the American school has been the slavish devotion of teachers and administrators to the use of textbooks.

The era of textbook teaching is on the way out. Textbooks are, as a whole, committed to the perpetuation of knowledge. In recent years they have been less able to fulfill this function than formerly. In many subjects, especially the social studies, new knowledge is being amassed so fast that parts of textbooks become obsolete between the time they are written and the time they leave the printing press. A recent popular sixth grade social studies series printed in September and released in February contained no mention of nine African nations which had been formed within that period, nor were any of the maps of Africa up to date. This state of affairs puts great responsibility on the teacher, where it has rightfully belonged all along. Too many courses of study in schools have been determined from textbooks and not from the needs of the children or the needs of any particular community.

Oscar Handlin points out that the textbook is often an obstacle rather than an aid to learning. The improvements in layout and format in recent texts have not been balanced by similar improvements in content. The result has been an endless cycle of unimaginative and imitative material which leaves little room for creative learning.[2]

The few exceptions which Mr. Handlin mentions may be described as follows:

(1) Many social studies textbooks have performed an excellent service in the manner by which they have developed map skills.

(2) Some textbooks have made contributions to children's critical thinking by the manner in which they have presented material and posed thought-provoking problems within the text.

(3) A few social studies textbooks have helped children to develop *some* social skills by suggesting kinds of activities which really place children in social situations requiring social competence.

(4) Textbooks have made possible the organization of large amounts of material ahead of time, thus making the research job of the teacher an easy one.

(5) Textbooks have placed a great deal of concrete information at the immediate disposal of children and teachers.

(6) Textbooks have provided for continuity of learning from year to year.

(7) Textbooks have provided teachers with excellent visual aids for teaching.

(8) Some textbooks have presented material in such a way as to develop basic values in children.

By and large, however, textbooks have not done much to promote creative learning or creative teaching. Many publishers will argue that this is not their function. This may be true. On the other hand, any agency which has such a great impact on the educational system of a country and "earns its keep" in creating that impact has a moral obligation to society to be sure its aims are consistent with those of the school and that the books with which it floods the schools contribute to the maximum development of the school program. The time-worn argument that publishers must give teachers what they want is inconsistent with the concept that education is the process that produces change.

Teachers can use textbooks creatively and many do. But by

[2] O. Handlin, "Textbooks That Don't Teach," *Atlantic Monthly*, CC, No. 6 (1957), pp. 110–13.

and large, it is not an easy task when most textbooks are so unrelated to real learning and are so uncreative in their presentation. George Stoddard says this about textbook teaching:

> Now we know that memory has a part to play in learning: speaking any language, including our own, involves a vast number of correlated impressions on call. The trouble is that in textbooks far removed from original sources, we are fed fragments that conform neither to the logical demands of an intellectual discipline nor to the psychological needs of the learner. Devoid of form, many a textbook renders its authors wholly unexciting. Our search for creativity therefore demands a new role for the textbook—a lesser one in the totality of the school day, but a deeper one. Its main purpose should be introductory. It should stir the student to ask, and find the answers for, key questions. It should send him to original readings, experiments and experiences not otherwise occurring to him; it should transport him across the barrier of words to sights, sounds, feeling, and emotions. Such a work viewed as map, ticket, or guidebook is defensible; not itself creative, a good textbook can show the way to creativeness.[3]

This author believes that the textbook of the future *must* be guided by the concept stated above by Stoddard. It is his firm belief that textbooks (and so-called workbooks) *can* be designed to take an active part in the creative development of teachers *and* children.

There are many ways in which this can be accomplished. Several are cited in the book on social studies in this series.

8. *Administration and School Policy:* Hundreds of young teachers currently graduating from teacher training institutions will go into new positions, eager and enthusiastic, only to be told by their chief administrator, "Now you can forget all those things you learned in college—we have to be practical here." The implication is, of course, that all the new knowledge and new skills which the young teacher has just learned have no value in the regular classroom. This attitude has kept many teachers from becoming more creative, or even more professional, over the past years. The administrator who is prompted by such an attitude is a very uncreative person himself. He is, in a sense, a victim of his own uncreative training and his own inability to rise above the

---

[3] G. Stoddard, "Creativity in Education," in *Creativity and Its Cultivation*, ed. Harold H. Anderson (New York: Harper and Brothers, 1959), p. 182.

accepted patterns of the past or the criticisms of the school patrons. Such an administrator provides little professional leadership. It takes a very strong, dedicated and skilled young teacher to survive his pressures and his criticisms. Such administrators must understand the importance of developing creativity in the individual child—and must also come to realize that the same conditions which a teacher sets in a classroom to develop creativity in the children are the ones he must set in his school building to develop creativity in his teachers.

GOOD TEACHING AND CREATIVE TEACHING

My lesson in Miss Walker's third grade was not a "bad" lesson. I remember how pleased I was to receive a "B" for it. In view of the understanding of method at that time I had turned in an acceptable performance. I had kept order, I had presented my material well, and I had drawn my lesson to a logical conclusion. In the evaluation which followed, both Miss Walker and my supervisor complimented me on my first performance.

It was good, but it was not creative. Creative teaching, as we are beginning to realize, is something quite different from the teaching described above. To fully understand this difference it will be necessary to review the emerging concepts of creativity— and see how these concepts apply to creative methodology.

SUMMARY

Creative teaching is a unique and special method of teaching based on a set of sound principles discovered through research studies. Creative teaching demands creative teachers. To develop creative teachers our concepts of good teaching must include the fact that teaching is not a mimetic process but a creative one. The challenge to produce creative teachers is as pressing in our teacher-training institutions as is the challenge to produce creative children in our classrooms. Creative teaching cannot result from imitation— it must be individual, unique, different. Teachers must see themselves as "bridging engineers" who translate the basic principles derived from research into classroom methodology.

There are currently several barriers to creative teaching which must be removed. Chief among these are: lack of intelligence, excessive conformity to predetermined methods of teaching or teaching plans, overplanning for classroom teaching, making the same plans for all children, the excessive use of stereotyped questions, the improper use of gimmicks, the overuse of the textbook as a teaching device, the inability on the part of teachers and administrators to differentiate between research and the opinion of the experts, and the attitude and practices of the school administrator who does not recognize the value of unique performance among his personnel.

In the following chapters we will more clearly define the "methods" of creative teaching.

To the College Student

Do you remember being subjected to lessons such as the one described in this chapter? Can you remember how you felt about them? Can you remember teachers who took a more creative approach to teaching and can you remember how you felt about them, also? Discuss various dull or exciting projects, lessons and teachers you had in school and begin to make a list of the basic differences between stereotyped and creative teaching.

Make a "Zouch". Immediately you will ask, "What is a zouch?" Obviously there is no such thing. Nevertheless, play with the idea—what does a zouch mean to you? Have each member of the class make one and bring it to class on a specified date. This assignment will help you to see how creative your class members are—and how one stimulus can evoke a variety of individual responses.

Collect some recent books which describe methods of teaching. Evaluate them in terms of whether they are dogmatic cookbooks for teaching or whether they inspire and stimulate the teacher to bring her own ideas and her own personality to the teaching art.

Discuss this topic in class: Plan Book: A Help or a Hindrance?

To the Classroom Teacher

Examine the lessons you taught most recently—how many different techniques did you use? How many were new and how many had you used time and time again? Which lessons evoked creative responses from the children? Which left them bored? Which left *you* bored? Reconstruct the poorest lesson you taught and see if you can think of new and creative ways to teach it.

I cheated the children in Miss Walker's Third Grade. The reader will ask, "How can the teaching of handwriting be creative when good handwriting means conforming to predetermined patterns?" Granted, good handwriting practice involves a great deal of conformity, but the TEACHING of it need not. Make a list of the basic principles behind the teaching of all handwriting today—and then see if you can apply them through a creative lesson in handwriting, teaching for legibility and efficiency in writing.

Make a list of the actual blocks to creativity you encounter in your schoolroom situation. Honestly consider each situation you listed—is there anything *you* can do about it? If so jot down ideas you might try out. Make sure the blocks really exist and are not legends passed along by other teachers who are always telling you what you can't do.

To the College Student and
the Classroom Teacher

Each chapter of this book is introduced with a quotation from a person who has studied the topic of creativity. Read these quotations carefully. Note that they represent viewpoints from many walks of life. From the short quotes can you detect any common thread of meaning running through the definitions of creativity? What are some of the unique ideas contributed by these experts?

There is a film named *Fiddle Dee Dee* which you should see.[4] After you see it ask yourself these questions:

• Have you ever seen anything like it before? How did it make you feel? What was your reaction to it?

• Try to analyze what you did while you were seeing this film. Did you try to get a story from it? Did you try to make sense out of it? Did you try to get a message from it? If you did or didn't, why? For those who didn't, why could you not accept it just as it was? Do you feel your reaction to this film has any indication as to your ability to be flexible? To see relationships? To be inventive or to analyze or abstract? Talk this over in class.

[4] *Fiddle Dee Dee.*—4 min., col., National Film Bureau, Canada.

Another film of similar nature which you might enjoy is *Hen Hop*.[5] Here are some films you will enjoy that will help reconstruct some of your concepts about creativity:

Color—6 min., col., Encyclopaedia Britannica Films

Elements of Design: Composition—11 min., bw., Young America Films

Elements of Design: Light and Shade—11 min., bw., Young America Films

Let's Try Choral Reading—10 min., bw., Young America Films

The Loon's Necklace—10 min., col., Encyclopaedia Britannica Films

After you have seen these films think through some of these problems:

- Which ones impressed you as being informative to the degree that they changed your way of thinking?

- Which one would you consider to be a creative masterpiece in its own right?

- Which one showed best a truly creative classroom teaching situation? What were the teacher's objectives in this film? How was the teacher developing creativity in the children according to the criteria set up for creative teaching in this book? How did the teacher set conditions for creativity to take place?

- Did any of these films change your concept of creativity? How?

Creativity has been referred to in this chapter as non-conformity. Are there times when children and adults must conform? Decide when these instances are. When should a teacher teach for conformity and when for creativity?

List ten great creative contributions to our culture in the past ten years. Consider all vocations and professions.

Reconstruct the lesson taught by the author in this chapter so that some of the basic principles of creative teaching are included: what would be a more creative way of teaching the letter "A"?

Design a format for a lesson plan which differs from the one in Miss Walker's grade in that it considers individual needs, engages children in the learning process, makes use of basic principles for teaching handwriting and draws on the creative abilities of children.

[5] *Hen Hop*.—5 min., col., International Film Bureau.

SELECTED BIBLIOGRAPHY

Bryson, L. "Training for Creativity," *School Arts*, LX (September 1960), 5–8.

Bulletin of Bureau of School Service: Creativity in its Classroom Context, XXXVI, No. 4. Lexington: College of Education, University of Kentucky, 1963.

Burkhart, R. C. *Spontaneous and Deliberate Ways of Learning*. Scranton, Pa.: International Textbook, 1962.

Carlson, Ruth K. "Stimulating Creativity in Children and Youth," *Elementary English*, XXXIX (1961), 165–69.

Dale, Edgar. "Education for Creativity," *The News Letter*, XXX, No. 3 (Dec. 1964).

Deutsch, K. W. "Creativity in a Scientific Civilization," in *Changing Attitudes in a Changing World*. New York: Bank Street College of Education Publications, 1958.

Dunkel, H. B. "Creativity and Education," *Education Theory*, XI (1961), 209–16.

Forsuhind, J. E. "Inquiry into the Nature of Creative Teaching," *Journal of Education*, 143 (1962), 72–82.

McKinnon, Donald W. "What Makes a Person Creative?" *Saturday Review* (Feb. 1962) 15–17.

Mead, M. *A Creative Life For Your Children*. Washington: U. S. Department of Health Education and Welfare, 1962.

Miel, Alice, ed. *Creativity in Teaching: Invitations and Instances*. Belmont, California: Wadsworth Publishing Company, Inc., 1961.

Mueller, G. and Applezweig, M. J. "A Motivational Factor in Conformity," *Journal Abnormal Psychology*, LV (1957), 114–20.

Osborn, Alex F. *Applied Imagination* (3rd ed.). New York: Charles Scribner's Sons, 1963.

———. *Your Creative Power: How to Use Imagination*. New York: Charles Scribner's Sons, 1949.

Parnes, S. J. "Can Creativity Be Increased?" *Art Education*, III, No. 1 (Fall, 1961), 39–46.

Parnes, S. J. and Harding, H. F. (eds.). *A Source Book for Creative Teaching*. New York: Charles Scribner's Sons, 1962.

Smith, James A. *Creativity: Its Nature and Nurture*. Syracuse: School of Education, Syracuse University, 1964.

Stein, Morris I. and Heinze, Shirley. *Creativity and the Individual*. Glencoe, Illinois: The Free Press, 1960.

Torrance, E. P. *Guiding Creative Talent*. Englewood Cliffs, N. J.: Prentice-Hall Inc., 1962.

Torrance, E. P. (ed.). *Creativity*. Minneapolis: University of Minnesota, Center for Continuation Study of the General Extension Division, 1959.

*C*reativeness cannot be taught; it can only be released
and guided. This, in essence, is the job of the teacher
—to release inner power into productive outer channels.[1]

——————————————————————————MAUREE APPELGATE

[1] Mauree Appelgate, *Helping Children Write* (White Plains, New York: Row, Peterson and Co., 1954), p. 1.

VIII——Setting Conditions for Creative Teaching

CREATIVITY, as such, cannot be taught. It is not a subject or a skill which can be learned like history or demonstrated like baseball. It is an inborn, developmental quality, like love, and can only be developed. Various aspects of creative thinking and doing can be modified through learning to the degree that all learning can be modified. But, because creativity is a quality already present in every individual, it needs to be coddled to help it develop. The uncreative children in our schools today are living testimony to the degree to which it can be killed off easily. Once it appears on the surface its reappearance can be assured by use of all those techniques which cause behavior to reappear. But it does not appear unless certain conditions are present which cause it to come forth. The problem, then, seems to be to get it to appear so the teacher can work with it, and by re-enforcement stimulate its reappearance—in other words *set conditions for creativity.*

Many writers in all fields of creativity have stressed the importance of proper conditions for creative development. Eyring, speaking from the scientist's viewpoint, has this to say about conditions for creativity:

> Even the gifted individual requires a stimulating environment, including freedom from distractions which deflect attention from the question at issue, and freedom from an authoritarian society which prevents unbiased inquiry. He profits likewise from congenial surroundings and stimulating company. He should preferably be completely at peace with the world except for the violent conflicts characterizing the problem engaging his attention. Thus he needs to be independent of all types of vicious circles which deflect attention from the problem at hand.[2]

Hilgard, in speaking about conditions for creativity, says:

> The conditions for creativity will have to be carefully nourished if we want more creativity to be demonstrated. All of our evidence shows that we must keep search alive, and we must allow sensitivity to new ideas, perhaps tolerating a little foolishness. We must not develop critical abilities to the point that anything unproven is stupid or that anything weak is altogether wrong. We must not insist upon conformity or we will end with traditionalists rather than with innovators.[3]

Rogers states the following as conditions which foster constructive creativity.

> My experience in psychotherapy leads me to believe that by setting up conditions of psychological safety and freedom, we maximize the likelihood of an emergence of constructive creativity.[4]

VonFange makes this observation about creativity as applied to industry:

> Creativity is discouraged in an environment where everyone is assigned enough activities to fill each working week—simply because supervisors can more easily observe, correct, and measure physical results in terms of jobs completed. It is difficult to manage thinking, and even more difficult to measure it; therefore, supervisors may be loath to allow any time for such abstract activity. As a consequence, they cannot accept any innovations, since applied creative effort demands time and thought.[5]

[2] H. Eyring, "Scientific Creativity," in *Creativity and Its Cultivation*, ed. Harold H. Anderson (New York: Harper and Brothers, 1959), p. 4.

[3] E. Hilgard, "Creativity and Problem-Solving," in *Creativity and Its Cultivation*, pp. 179–80.

[4] G. Rogers, "Toward a Theory of Creativity," in *Creativity and Its Cultivation*, p. 78.

[5] E. VonFange, *Professional Creativity* (Englewood Cliffs, N.J.: Prentice-Hall, Inc., 1959), pp. 76–77.

In tackling the question, "Can Creativity Be Developed," Guilford[6] points out that students can be exposed to experiences and problems in all areas to develop creative thinking. Much depends on how subject matter is taught and the attitudes of the teacher who must understand the nature of creative performances, as well as her ability to select appropriate materials.

Meadow and Parnes[7] experimented with creative problem solving and concluded that a creative problem solving course produces a significant increase in certain abilities associated with practical creativity. This research indicates that creativity *can* be developed under the proper conditions.

Maltzman[8] agrees that the way to foster originality is to re-enforce such behavior when it appears. It may not appear, however. He believes that the fundamental problem in the training of originality is to devise methods for increasing its occurrence in diverse situations in the first place, thereby permitting re-enforcement.

In attempting to find the effects of motivation on training for creativity, Torrance[9] found that children reacted more favorably to motivation which produced ideas with quality in the first three grades while in the fourth and sixth grades children tended to produce ideas in greater quantity. The results of his studies were not conclusive but may indicate that primary grade children tend to be less inhibited when motivated to create under certain situations than intermediate grade children, and that there *may* be differences in the way they create.

Torrance and his colleagues[10] have devised numerous work books designed to develop creative thinking and creative writing.

[6] J. P. Guilford, "Can Creativity Be Developed?" *Education Digest*, XXIV (December 1958), pp. 49–51.

[7] A. Meadow and S. J. Parnes, "Evaluation of Training in Creative Problem Solving," *Journal of Applied Psychology*, XLIII (June 1959), pp. 189–94.

[8] I. Maltzman, "On the Training of Originality," *Psychological Review*, LVII (1960), pp. 229–42.

[9] E. P. Torrance, *Explorations in Creative Thinking in the Early School Years: II. An Experiment in Training and Motivation* (Minneapolis: Bureau of Educational Research, University of Minnesota, 1959), pp. 30–31.

[10] R. E. Myers and E. Paul Torrance, *Can You Imagine: A Book of Ideas for Children in the Primary Grades* (New York: Ginn & Co., 1965).
———, *Invitations to Speaking and Writing Creatively* (New York: Ginn & Co., 1965).

Results obtained from the use of these materials is encouraging. These men also used certain taped materials which were designed to put children through a "warm-up" process and to make them alert to the creative process. These materials are at present being tested and are available for general use.

That specific conditions are an aid to creative production cannot be disputed. Rugg tells again and again in his accounts of the habits of creative individuals how many of them chose a specific place or a specific room in which to write or paint because that particular spot seemed to agitate their own creative production. I have found this to be true of children also. We had a piano in our classroom. I placed it in a corner and added a screen to shelter the corner completely. In this little shelter I placed a table on which there was a typewriter and some writing materials. By it I placed a chair. A sign on the screen said, "Writer's Corner." I was amazed at the times I found children in this shelter completely absorbed in writing. It was understood that only one at a time would use the Writer's Corner—and there was always a waiting list. Much of what they wrote in this cubicle was of deeper emotional and personal content than what they wrote in class.

CONDITIONS FOR CREATIVITY

The conditions which tend to develop creativity may be placed under five categories: (1) intellectual conditions; (2) physical conditions; (3) social-emotional conditions; (4) psychological conditions; and (5) educational conditions. By conditions this author means those techniques or environmental stimuli designed to evoke original behavior, uncommon responses and a steady flow of ideas. These conditions have been culled from research, from the opinions of recognized experts and from accounts written by creative teachers who described their particular motivational plans.

All through this series, the author will make reference to two

———, *Teachers Manual for Invitations to Speaking and Writing Creatively* (New York: Ginn & Co., 1965).
———, *Invitations to Thinking and Doing* (New York: Ginn & Co., 1965).
———, *Teachers Manual for Invitations to Thinking and Doing* (New York: Ginn & Co., 1965).

basic types of conditions or experiences used in provoking creative behavior: the natural type and the contrived type. Natural conditions are those which happen naturally in any classroom when the teacher is quick enough and sharp enough to utilize the situation for the development of some creative work. The story of the dandelions on page 25 is an example of such a natural experience. A contrived experience is one where the teacher plans a lesson with the specific intent of plunging the children into a problem where creative thinking and creative production results. An example of this type is demonstrated in the lesson about the Valentine poem on page 16.

Both natural and contrived experiences may fall within the five categories.

INTELLECTUAL CONDITIONS

To set conditions for the emergence of creative thinking and creative development the teacher will: (1) Provide opportunities and resources for a great deal of knowledge and a great many skills to be learned through convergent thinking processes. Although divergent thinking processes develop the creative functions of the intellect, every individual must first have vast amounts of knowledge, great numbers of facts and many thinking skills at his fingertips to apply them to divergent thinking processes.

Harold Rugg has stated it in this fashion:

> No man, be he artist or scientist, technologist or philosopher, will be successful either in thinking directly or in thinking aside in his search for the unknown, unless his mind is equipped with all the needed materials with which to think: with that multitude of facts, principles, theories, that might contain the one stimulus needed to precipitate the new idea. He must know a vast deal about the right things. Not just know a lot, but know the specially related things required to set off the particular spark. It is conscious preparation by deliberate manipulation of concepts into close juxtaposition that gives the greatest promise of permitting the spark of recognition to be ignited.[11]

(2) Provide many instances when the learning and skills of children may be applied to divergent thinking processes. The implication here is that knowledge, concepts, facts, and principles

---

[11] Harold Rugg, *Imagination: An Inquiry into the Sources and Conditions that Stimulate Creativity* (New York: Harper and Row, 1963), pp. 11–12.

83325

will not be learned solely for their own sake, but will be learned to solve problems. The teacher will constantly build on the experiential backgrounds of the children, placing them in problem-solving situations where past experiences may be utilized.

Convergent thinking processes may well be the means by which the necessary tension is built for creative production. Divergent thinking processes add a new dimension to convergent thinking: convergent thinking processes help the individual to know what is; divergent thinking processes help him to know what is to be. When convergent thinking is overused, it can keep an individual from thinking about what is to be.

(3) Develop many open-ended learning situations. Facts will be learned as part of the solution to problems which in themselves have no absolute solution. An example of the open-ended learning situation which calls for a mustering of facts to arrive at a logical solution is given on page 106. The traditional teacher years ago would have had the children memorize the populations of each state. In the open-ended situation described on page 106, the teacher shows the class a map on which populations of the states are drawn. She says, "Last year two of our greatest manufacturing states lost population, and the three fastest growing states were a desert state (Nevada), a swamp state (Florida) and a very mountainous state (California). Now, why do you suppose this is so?" Children, in trying to reach a logical answer to this question must gather facts, evaluate, and think creatively as they put these facts into new patterns.

The essential difference in the closed, convergent intellectual processes and the open, divergent intellectual processes is that in the one, the teacher can fairly well predict the outcome. She can plan to teach addition of like denominators in fractions at 11:00 A.M. on Tuesday and be fairly certain that by 11:30 all but Joey, Phyllis, Albert and Renee will have mastered the process. These children, she knows, will require special help because they are slow. Thelma, Vicki and John will need extra stimulation because they are so bright so she will plan more work for them. This is closed, convergent learning.

In the open, divergent intellectual processes the teacher cannot predict the outcome of her teaching: she must set conditions by motivating the children to the experience at hand, taking them through that experience with her up to a certain point, and then letting them go. In open-ended learning, it is essential that, at one place in the learning process, the children face the unknown by themselves. The product from this kind of teaching is unpredictable —and the source of the creative product is also unpredictable. It may come from the slow as well as the bright child.

(4) Plan teaching situations, questions and discussions in such a way that *all* children think *all* of the time. The question-answer, stimulus-response type of guessing game will not be the predominant mode of teaching. Problems and questions presented will not be of the factual nature, but will be of the type that involves critical, creative divergent thinking processes so all minds are at work and contributing to the problem at hand.

A simple illustration of this type of problem situation is the lesson with the dandelions on page 26. In this instance each child is encouraged to think of more and more ways to describe the dandelions. All are thinking all the time; minds are not placed in low gear waiting for one particular child to be called on.

(5) Utilize *all* areas of the curriculum to provide content and situations for the development of creativity in children (see Chapter X).

In discussing the process of creativity it was pointed out that many times a problem haunts the individual for days. Many writers have told how the flash of insight which gave the solution to the problem seemed to come when the mind was in a semi-conscious state—either a daze, a trance or a dream. Teachers ought not to be too upset if children cannot arrive at creative solutions to problems the first time they are posed. A long incubation period may be necessary, or a period of involvement before anyone in the class gains the flash of insight needed for the solution to the problem. Sometimes it is wise to allow the children to mull over the problem for several days.

(6) Teach to develop the specific intellectual skills needed in the process of creating, such as those outlined by Guilford, Marksberry and others and reported in Chapter VI. These skills will include the ability to think deductively, to see relationships, to pass judgment and make decisions, to think critically and creatively, to develop associations, to defer judgment, to abstract and to construct symbols, to solve problems, the ability to adapt, to modify, to magnify, to minify, to rearrange, to reverse, to classify and to contrast. Methods of developing these skills will be discussed in

Chapter IX and in Book IV: *Setting Conditions For Creative Teaching of the Social Studies*, and on page 162.

PHYSICAL CONDITIONS

Conditions for creative development may be greatly enhanced by proper attention to certain physical aspects of the child's environment.

(1) *Room arrangement:* If creativity is developed through exploring, manipulating, discovering, problem-solving and working with new materials, it becomes obvious that the classroom must be a workshop with many materials available. One effective way to provide physical stimuli for creative production is to use the idea of "centers" in the classroom. Under this plan different parts of the room are designated for various activities. The physical arrangement makes it possible for group or individual work to take place with a minimum amount of furniture-moving and material-gathering.

Each room should have an art center where paints, scissors, paste, construction paper, clay, brushes, and other materials are easily available. There should be an easel in the art center—even in the upper grades. If the room has a sink, it is wise to locate the art center near the sink.

If the room should have a piano, a music center could be built around it. If possible, a phonograph should be available in the music center. A simple xylophone or marimba should be handy for creating songs. If they are inaccessible, tuned glasses or flower pots will do. Song books, a pad of blank music paper, and any instruments that can be obtained (such as rhythm instruments) should be kept in this center. Bongo drums or simple musical toys can be the impetus for much creative work.

In the primary grades, teachers will want a block corner, a homemaking corner and a construction corner.

All children benefit from rooms which have a science center with a terrarium or aquarium. In this center simple science materials should be kept along with specimens brought in by the children (see Book VII).

Each room should have a construction bench or simple workbench with a vise, some nails, hammers, saws, chisels, brace and bits, and pieces of wood.

There should be a center where children may have fun with words, even if it is only a shelf for language materials—a word center or vocabulary center. In this center there should be some attractive dictionaries and books dealing with words such as *Ounce, Dice, Trice,*[12] and *On Beyond Zebra.*[13]

Somewhere in the room there should be a research center. In it should be encyclopedias, reference books, atlases, globes, almanacs, maps, books of information and reference, a radio and, if possible, a television set (see Book IV).

Of course there must also be a library—a place where children may exchange their own books and have available to them many trade books and textbooks for reading (see Book III).

Last, but most important of all, every classroom should have movable seats *that are moved.* In planning for a school day it is as important to plan the movement of the furniture as it is to plan the studies and activities of the children. The teacher will need to keep in mind a mental picture of the children's movements from one experience to another during the school day to keep the movement of the furniture at a minimum. She should check this "movement" plan with the children in the planning period at the beginning of each day.

With movable seats those human relationships become possible from which true creative experiences develop. Grouping of all kinds is possible with movable furniture, and a large space for free movement can be quickly obtained by moving the furniture out of the way.

The classroom should be well lighted and well ventilated. Most modern schools keep fluorescent lights turned on all day long to assure the proper lighting on each desk. Glare and contrast in dark and light should be avoided to prevent eyestrain. Seats and tables should be adjusted to the size of the pupil. Adjustable chalk boards, walls covered with cork board, peg board areas and windows looking out on interesting scenes make the atmosphere highly conducive to creating.

Above all, the classroom should be attractive. Materials need to be carefully arranged. The teacher should be sensitive to color and keep the color in the room blending and pleasant. Brash and

[12] Alstair Reid, *Ounce, Dice, Trice* (Boston: Little, Brown and Co., 1958).
[13] Dr. Seuss, *On Beyond Zebra* (New York: Random House, 1955).

conflicting colors often create unconscious irritations in children. The teacher should be a good housekeeper, keeping the total picture of the room in her mind so it does not become too cluttered or dirty. Too much confusion will often distract many children to the point where they find it difficult to concentrate—although we do know also, that some types of disorder challenge creative children. Lack of a modern, beautiful building need not necessarily mean lack of a beautiful, stimulating and creative environment. In fact, the challenge to the teacher who has inherited a dingy, poorly-equipped classroom is even greater than that to her more fortunate sisters. The chances are great that her children, more than others, need the enriching environment necessary to foster creativity and learning. And the techniques this teacher employs to create such an environment the children themselves may later employ to enrich their own home surroundings.

Many teachers have guided creative development by having one cupboard in the classroom stocked with a few attractive yet inexpensive vases of various shapes, some colorful pieces of cloth for arrangements, a few attractive picture frames collected from some attic and refinished for various purposes, a few figurines— often made from papier-mâché by the pupils, some chicken wire that can be wadded into vases for holding flower arrangements, a few pieces of attractive driftwood, a few simply woven rush or yarn mats, a candle or two and a box of odds and ends of attractive paper, yarn and twine. These, of course, can be supplemented by a few nice pieces of pottery and some nice fabrics if there is money available. It was to such a center that I sent Marion the day she brought me the dandelions (see page 25).

A teacher facing a group of children at the beginning of a term needs to examine a multitude of ways she can guide creative development through the use of the schoolroom environment. She can utilize the colors the children wear in their clothing to develop artistic values providing she does not jeopardize the status of some children and exploit others. The arrangement of her bulletin boards, the storage of materials, the placement of furniture all relate to the basic problem of building organization and relationships in the children.

Children have a first-hand experience with table arrangements.

(2) *Availability of Materials:* Creative production cannot always be preplanned. Though it is true that the teacher can set conditions for a natural or contrived creative experience, much of what is creative comes from capitalizing on a particular stimulus incidentally—as it comes up in the classroom. Many opportune moments are lost when materials are not available. In modern classrooms cupboards and shelves are plentiful so materials may be placed where children can easily reach them. A short unit on the arrangement of the room at the beginning of the year gives children the opportunity to put things in place where they can find them without asking the teacher. Such a unit is described in *Setting Conditions for Creative Teaching of Social Studies.*

Some materials should be ready for use at all times as we have seen above. These would include such items as paper and pencils, chart paper, maps, globes, flo pens, tape recorders, phonographs, simple musical instruments and reference books. Others should be available but the teacher and children will need to plan schedules so they can be used at a time when children are not disturbed. These materials would include saws, hammers, noisy toys, science equipment, the phonograph, the piano and tuned glasses.

Children should *know* their classroom and feel free to move about it. In addition they should know their school environment well so materials can be easily located outside the classroom. They should know where the bats, balls, nets and play equipment are located. They should know where they can borrow musical instruments, science materials, additional textbooks, paintings, pictures, audio-visual equipment and any other material that might be needed for any particular lesson or experience.

Children obtain a great deal of security if they understand exactly how school equipment is to be signed out for classroom use. Any rules that must be applied to the use of equipment should be explained so the children see the necessity for such rules, and then they should be enforced. Committees to take responsibility for the borrowing, use and return of the equipment should be set up by the children.

They should know when certain areas of the school environment are available to them: the playground areas, the gymnasium, the science laboratory, the art or music studios, the cafeteria and auditorium.

They should also know when consultants or special teachers are available for help. More will be said in later books about the use of the art teacher and other consultants but it should be mentioned here that so-called special teachers serve little purpose when they are not available to help children when they are needed.

The availability of a variety of materials encourages children to solve problems for they know where to get *some* help immediately when the problem arises.

Studies by Torrance[14] and his colleagues indicate that creativity and inventiveness are encouraged when children are allowed to manipulate objects and ideas. These researchers feel that it would be desirable to encourage and implement the natural tendencies of children to manipulate objects and ideas in order to encourage inventiveness. In the books which follow the author has attempted to apply this basic principle in demonstrating how creativity can be encouraged by manipulating ideas, materials, objects and living conditions in the classroom.

[14] E. P. Torrance, Frank B. Baker and John E. Bower, "Explorations in Creative Thinking in the Early School Years," *Research Memoranda* (Minneapolis: Bureau of Educational Research, University of Minnesota, 1959).

(3) *The Organization of the Class:* The manner in which a class is organized contributes to creative development. Children will not be relaxed nor will they feel free to contribute their ideas in an autocratic situation where the structure of the classroom is dependent on leadership of the teacher alone. Children learn to make their individual contributions and learn to make group decisions by practicing these skills in a democratically run classroom. They learn to respect others and to share ideas when they have had the opportunity to listen to each other's ideas, and enjoy the glow that comes from having successfully solved a group problem.

In a permissive, creative and democratic classroom children and teacher plan the day's work together. Children at times work as well in small groups as in one large group. They share ideas and materials. Children learn from each other as well as from the teacher. Children are motivated to the degree that they can carry on when the teacher must leave the room on an errand. Individual needs are respected and planned for. Individual differences are honored and encouraged, for creativity means individuality and the class must be organized so the teacher can capitalize on the different talents that each child brings to the classroom situation.

In Book IV a detailed description is given of the organization of such a class.

The "formal" schoolroom quickly destroys the joy of creating and individuality because it is wrong to be different according to the standards set by the teacher. For although the drive to create is as strong within children as the drive for status, the drive to be loved is stronger and is a more basic need. And children, seeking emotional and psychological security, will quickly conform to the teacher's wishes in order not to provoke her disfavor or ridicule. It is this same social pressure from other influential individuals in the child's life, and later his society itself, that makes for a nation of conformists.

New patterns of organization such as the departmentalized "middle school" and the homogeneous grouping of children in nongraded reading groups are causing great concern among people who see them as deterrents to the development of creativity. The short periods of time each child spends with many teachers does not provide for the on-going development of the creative process such as the self-contained classroom does. The development of creativity *can* take place in these organizational plans to some degree, depending as it does in all cases on the teachers involved. But the chances are less because of the *number* of teachers involved.

SOCIAL-EMOTIONAL CONDITIONS

Social-emotional conditions which develop creativity are many:

(1) rewarding varied kinds of talents and creative achievements; (2) helping children recognize the value of their creative talents; (3) developing creative acceptance of realistic limitations in a problem situation; (4) being sensitive to the needs of children, stressing and praising differences, uniqueness and originality rather than likeness and commonness; (5) accepting "silly" ideas as a sign of creative thinking; (6) helping all children to accept the creative child; (7) developing an atmosphere that is permissive to the extent that children are free to experiment, explore and make mistakes; (8) developing an appreciation for creativity in the classroom; (9) avoiding the equation of difference with mental illness and delinquency; (10) modifying the misplaced emphasis on sex roles; (11) helping highly creative children become less objectionable; (12) helping to reduce the isolation of highly creative children; and (13) helping highly creative children cope with anxieties and fears.

The Minnesota studies show that competition in grades one to six increases fluency, flexibility and originality in creative writing tasks. Practice and "warm-up" did not completely eliminate the advantage achieved by competition. These studies also show that individuals tend to achieve along those lines in which they are rewarded. When rewarded for originality, sixth grade children produced about twice as many original ideas as when they were rewarded for quantity regardless of quality.

These studies also show that if one member of a group is superior to the others in creative thinking abilities, he almost always experiences pressure to reduce his productivity and originality or both, and is frequently not given credit for the positive contribution to the group's success.[15]

Homogeneous grouping for tasks requiring creative problem

---

[15] E. P. Torrance, "Education and Creativity" in Taylor, Calvin W., *Creativity: Progress and Potential* (New York: McGraw-Hill, 1964), pp. 103–06.

solving reduces the social stress, enables less creative members to become more productive and increases the enjoyment of members.

These studies also indicate that urban cultures appear to be more intolerant of divergence than rural cultures. Children in special classes for the gifted seemed to be more tolerant of divergence than children in regular classes. Minority groups seem to feel rather strong pressure to conform to the larger society.

Taylor[16] has listed some social-emotional factors which act as inhibiting forces against creative development. His list includes: success-orientation (we are anti-failure); peer-orientation (pressures for conformity); sanctions against questioning and exploration; overemphasis or misplaced emphasis on sex roles; equating divergency with "abnormality"; our work-play dichotomy.

Removal of emphasis on these particular factors may do a great deal to provide a more suitable social atmosphere for creative development.

PSYCHOLOGICAL CONDITIONS

Psychological conditions which appear essential for the development of creativity may be conceived as follows: (1) a physically and mentally hygienic classroom as described above; (2) a permissive atmosphere based on certain underlying securities; (3) the proper motivation and tensions to agitate creative thinking and creative production; and (4) the proper attitude in the teachers and the school administrator towards creativity.

(1) *The physically and mentally hygenic classroom:* The physically healthy classroom has been described above and the mentally hygenic classroom will be described in the pages that follow. Torrance has listed the following as necessary conditions for the healthy functioning of the preconscious mental processes which produce creativity: (1) the absence of serious threat to self, the willingness to risk, (2) self-awareness—the ability to keep in touch with one's feelings, (3) self-differentiation—the ability to see self as being different from others, (4) both openness to the ideas of others and confidence in one's own perceptions of reality or one's own ideas and (5) mutuality in interpersonal relations—a balance between

---

[16] Calvin Taylor, *Creativity: Progress and Potential* (New York: McGraw-Hill, 1964), p. 98.

excessive quest for social relations and pathological rejection of them.[17]

Torrance[18] goes so far as to say that the repression of creativity in the classroom may create many problems in individuals. Among them are: a faulty or uncertain self-concept, certain learning disabilities, certain behavior problems, neurotic conflicts or even psychoses.

(2) *A permissive atmosphere:* Children must feel a certain freedom to explore, to test, to evaluate and to experiment. Even more, children must feel free to make mistakes; they must feel free to draw from their total life experience and to experiment with ideas, words and materials. "Silly" ideas must be accepted as creative ones; *new* solutions to problems must be sought as well as correct solutions; children must have the opportunity to share and learn from each other; there must be an "air of expectancy" toward creating.

But, permissiveness does not mean "laissez-faire". On the contrary it means a complete understanding on the part of the children and the teacher as to what behavior is permissible in the classroom so no single individual's rights and liberties are violated. A permissive atmosphere for all individuals can only exist when certain basic laws underlie the classroom organization. For instance, the teacher and the children must work out any basic rules to maintain order and proper working conditions. Children, through discussion, understand the purpose of these rules and abide by them. This is the type of necessary conformity needed to hold a society together. It can be comforting to creative children for they know exactly the limits and boundaries of their field of operation.

To develop a permissive atmosphere, the teacher must understand the creative process and the necessary human elements which foster it. She builds the creative "air of expectancy" mentioned above. This means she lets the children understand that she *expects* them to explore, experiment, try new ideas and be individuals. She helps them understand, by her own actions, that she has faith in them. She builds self-confidence in each child by letting

---

[17] E. P. Torrance, *Guiding Creative Talent* (Englewood Cliffs, N. J.: Prentice-Hall, Inc., 1962), pp. 143–44.

[18] *Ibid.*, pp. 125–41.

him know his capabilities and assuring him of her confidence in them. She accepts each child, expecting from him his best even though it does not measure up to someone else's. The teacher must *want* each child to be different and must place stress on differences.

Although the act of creating means that the creator pushes forth to explore the unknown, a certain amount of security or psychological safety is necessary to the child before this can happen. The shy, timid child is afraid to try new ventures. He has had too many disappointing experiences in the past. Now he is afraid of failure. He therefore withdraws from any new experience because he anticipates the unpleasantness of failure and wishes to avoid it.

"Failure" insecurity can only be replaced by "success" security. The teacher who inherits a shy child will find herself confronted with such statements as: "I don't like fingerpaint. It gets me dirty," or "I can't draw," or "I don't like to paint." Her first step is not to push the child into the situation for that would be a sure way of forcing him to withdraw further into himself. She will need to accept his excuses and then contrive situations where he can be successful until she leads him, gradually but firmly, back into the realm of self-confidence and success. Success experiences in any subject matter area are necessary if learning in that area is to continue.

Dr. Parnes, in his Instructor's Manual for the course in Creative Problem Solving says:

> Success in using the creative-problem-solving method depends a lot on your outlook.
>
> . . . failures should not lead to discouragement. They should be used as steppingstones instead of tombstones.[19]

(3) *The proper motivation and tensions to agitate creative thinking and creative production:* Motivation is a vital component of creativity and tensions are necessary to all learning. The motivation for creativity may supply the tensions which result in creative production.

In speaking of tension, Rugg says:

> Tension is perhaps the most meaningful and comprehensive concept. In using it, I shall imply both physiological and psycho-

---

[19] Sidney J. Parnes, *Instructors Manual for Semester Courses in Creative Problem-Solving* (Rev. ed.; Buffalo: Creative Education Foundation, 1963), p. 31.

logical connotations. The tension system of the organism is the key to the energy of creative imagination. The sparking concept is movement. Revealing itself in the irritability of protoplasm, it is as basic to the science of behavior as is the concept of motion to the physical sciences. It is its biological correlate.[20]

Through natural, everyday happenings and through premeditated, contrived plans, teachers can create situations which build up the tensions necessary for creative endeavor. Some examples of this tension-setting have already been explored and more will be given in the next chapter.

In order for the creative product to be a useful one, this must be "positive" tension. Positive tension is that which motivates or creates a need which results in a profitable or constructive end. The need to solve a problem creates tension. Solving the problem releases the tension and puts the child back into equilibrium.

Extreme negative tension can be detrimental to problem solving, or can result in learning which is not beneficial to the creator. Negative tension is that which is created out of excessive threat or fear rather than out of the desire to solve a problem. Fear of a nagging teacher, fear of failure, fear of poor grades or physical harm can create negative tension. Children pull in and become threatened under negative tension. Tension of this nature may be too emotionally packed to allow useful creative products to emerge.

(4) *The attitude of the teacher:* As a result of their research in creativity and intelligence, Getzels and Jackson[21] feel that what is most needed to develop creativity in the schools is a drastic change in parental and teacher attitudes toward giftedness and success.

Lack of understanding of the creative child and the creative process have contributed to the traditional image of the typical elementary school classroom. If creative development had been one of the objectives of education in the past, we could say that the typical image could not exist as it does today. This is why the first great change must be in the understanding and attitudes of the teacher. The teacher herself must work at being creative. The creative persons we are hoping to develop in our children should be

[20] Harold Rugg, *op. cit.*, p. 54.

[21] Jacob W. Getzels and Philip W. Jackson, *Creativity and Intelligence: Explorations with Gifted Students* (New York: John Wiley and Sons, Inc., 1962), p. 124.

exemplified in our teachers more than any other people. Teachers must be sensitive. They, above all others, must be understanding and able to see relationships. They must be interested in fostering individualism and raising cultural standards. They set the standards children are to imitate and paint the designs for living. They have an unlimited effect on the children by the incidental things they do as well as by the planned experiences they prepare for children.

Barkan[22] has shown that a teacher can develop creative thinking simply by the manner in which she talks to children. With practice, a teacher can develop this skill. Her main requisites are an understanding of the creative process and an understanding of how to recognize its development in her children.

That creative teachers develop creative children has already been demonstrated. The research of Torrance[23] has shown that the pupils of highly creative teachers produce more creative products than those of less creative teachers. The teacher is the most influential part of the classroom environment. Her personality, to a great extent, determines the amount of individuality that will go on in a schoolroom. She, herself, must have creative experiences and appreciate the inward joy of inventing something, and must be anxious for her pupils to experience similar joys and satisfactions.

The teacher who has not yet found joy in creating may do so at any point. Because creativity is a state of mind, she can only begin if she really has the desire to create and maintains a positive attitude toward her growth. A teacher who has used finger paint can understand the child's reaction to the slippery, gooey mass he so enjoys manipulating. The teacher who has painted a picture, shaped a ceramic object or woven a cloth can appreciate the effort a child puts into such work and can enjoy more the finished product. Teachers who do not know the joy of creating need not wait to discover it. They can do it along with their children and often find whole new vistas open to them to enrich their own living.

In order to free herself to be creative, a teacher should try to be relaxed; she must be confident in what she does; she must develop respect for each child and a willingness to listen to his ideas and plans; she must be courteous and patient with pupils and other

[22] M. Barkan, *Through Art to Creativity* (Boston: Allyn and Bacon, 1960).
[23] E. P. Torrance, *op. cit.*, pp. 71–72.

staff members. Her own mental health is important, for creativity cannot grow in an environment where the teacher is on the defensive and is threatened by inward insecurities.

Extremely important to the development of creativity is the attitude of the teacher toward discipline. Schools have confused discipline with order. Order is necessary for a good teaching situation, but not the military order seen in some classrooms. The concept of organization must replace that of military order. To a casual observer, a modern classroom with its groups of children working in varied activities may seem like chaos compared to orderly rows of children reading from the same textbook. But a more careful scrutiny of the situation will reveal that this chaos is really a highly-organized, well-planned working situation and that all the children are learning many things. In the modern school, where the child's need for bodily activity is recognized, the tensions created by the authoritarian climate of long ago are largely prevented by the informal atmosphere. Discipline problems, as they were once conceived, dissolve; for many of these problems were created by unreasonable demands on the children. The social climate of the classroom is of utmost importance in developing discipline which is self-discipline. The teacher attempts to remove hostilities and jealousies among children and encourage helpfulness and sharing. Children have a part in planning the work, in organizing the classroom and in being responsible for its functioning. They evaluate so-called "discipline" problems and set their own rules (see Book IV). Each act during the day, whether it be play or work, is determined by the joint effort to reach a goal.

In such a social climate, the teacher is a working member and guide in a group that has more independence than dependence. When teacher leaves the room, work goes on as usual. Erasers do not fly and the classroom does not disintegrate, for each child has a purpose and a job, and is not dependent on teacher to complete it. The ability of children to carry on constructively during the absence of the teacher may well be a test of the kind of discipline being developed and of her ability to develop creative human relationships.

To fully understand the concept of self-discipline it is necessary to consider the concept of independence. Independence implies maturity—a mature person is an independent one. Children mature to the extent that they are able to assume independent acts at various age levels. To deprive a child of his need for independence — or to teach him to cling to an adult for any act when he can carry it out alone, is depriving him of his right to mature. The more independence a child is able to assume in performing the tasks of his age and in thinking through his problems, the more capable he is of reasoning and appreciating, and of disciplining himself. Discipline and independence go hand-in-hand. A dependent child is always an immature one, and often a discipline problem. And a dependent child is rarely a creative one.

It is the duty of each teacher to guide each child toward this independence so he may function by himself as soon as possible. As long as teachers insist on telling children what to do children will not take the responsibility of doing it themselves. For years children have been patrolled in halls, marching to and from assembly and "basement," not learning to do it alone because teacher was present to put a child in line if he did not follow rules. Teenagers out of school often exhibit poor manners and lack of graciousness in public buildings because they are experiencing the use of these places alone for the first time. Responsibility should be built up during early years of the child so he becomes gracious and at ease in all situations. Children are anxious to learn the correct way of acting, but because adults treat them like babies they often act like babies. Children must be encouraged to become independent in the realization that self-discipline does not come when they do not take the responsibility for their behavior.

Closely allied to the concept of independence is the concept of obedience. So long as a child is merely being obedient he is acting in a way that he hopes will avoid displeasing another. He is not yet assuming responsibility for his own actions. It is the obligation of the teacher to help children progress from the immature level of obedience to the mature level of responsibility. At any given age a child may be functioning at an obedience level in some things and a responsibility level in others. An excessive and continued demand for obedience retards the growth of responsibility. In order to develop responsibility in children, obedience at the drop of a hat cannot be expected. Perhaps a balance can be struck between these traits, but it does not come easily. In a democracy, assuming responsibility and thinking for oneself are important. The slavish, automatic response to a dictatorial order is little better than deliberate and continued disobedience.

Obedience is often confused with respect, but to be obedient is not necessarily to be respectful. Adults feel threatened by children who are disobedient, for they fear the loss of authority. Adults must earn respect, they cannot demand it, and real obedience is based on respect for the judgment and opinion of an adult. A child who trusts his teacher, and has come to respect him and see him as a wise, honest person will accept his judgment in times when obedience is necessary even though the reason is remote or not understood by the child. The obedient child is the highly conforming child, and it is unlikely that he can develop his creative powers if he is over-conforming. We might safely say that obedience and creativity are at opposite ends of a continuum.

To build responsibility in children the teacher and parent must recognize the independence of the child in demanding to know, to reason or to refuse: a healthy sign that he is thinking for himself and is assuming responsibility for his own actions. Good classroom rapport, a healthy social climate and a freedom to express oneself eliminate unreasonable demands on children, and obedience as such is unnecessary in that the need for it seldom arises. Psychologically the child is free to think for himself.

(5) *The role of the administrator:*   On page 109 Chapter VII it was pointed out that administrative policy can be a deterrent to creative development. An administrator can help set conditions for creative teaching. Torrance[24] has listed the following ways of dealing with creative workers and keeping teams harmoniously productive. Although this list comes from research in business and industry, the items selected would also apply to school administrators.

The school administrator interested in guiding creative talent:

1. Lets teachers know that he respects creativity and creative teaching.
2. Uses some regular system to obtain teachers' ideas.
3. Tolerates disagreement with his ideas.
4. Encourages experimentation.
5. Avoids loading teachers with too many extra duties.
6. Makes it possible to try out new ideas without failure being "fatal."

[24] E. P. Torrance, *op. cit.*, p. 286.

7. Makes school atmosphere an exciting, adventurous one.

8. Avoids overemphasis on teamwork.

9. Holds meetings in which ideas are evaluated honestly.

10. Helps develop sound but exciting ideas from failure experiences.

11. Exposes teachers to the creative work of other teachers.

12. Makes it easy for new teachers to generate new ideas and stimulate the staff.

13. Facilitates communication between teachers in his school and teachers elsewhere working on related problems.

14. Occasionally questions established concepts and practices.

15. Carries on a continuous program of long-range planning.

16. Recognizes and tries to relieve tension when frustration becomes too severe.

17. Maintains frequent communication with individual teachers but lets them make most decisions alone.

Torrance goes on to state:

> From research in a variety of fields, we can also make some good guesses about what kind of person the creative administrator is.

He then lists his guesses as follows:

1. He is a man of curiosity and discontent. He is always asking, "Why did this happen?" or "What would happen if we did it this way?"

2. He is a man of unlimited enthusiasm for his job. He is restless, intense, strongly motivated, completely wrapped up in what he is doing.

3. He is a man with the talent of transmitting his enthusiasm to his associates. He creates an atmosphere of excitement and urgency.

4. He is flexible. He keeps an open mind and is willing to accept and use new information. He listens to new ideas and does not flatly dismiss ideas with "don't be ridiculous" or "we tried that before."

5. He is unorthodox and boldly questions conventional ideas. He is goal-oriented, *not* method-oriented. He is willing to pay the price in physical and mental labor to achieve goals and is impatient with anything that gets in the way.[25]

EDUCATIONAL CONDITIONS

Educational conditions are those which develop the reality that creative teaching is a *method* of teaching different from ordinary methods of teaching. These creative methods of teaching are governed by the basic principles of creative teaching described in the next chapter. They are also soundly rooted in what is currently known about the growth and development of children (especially creative growth), the basic accepted principles of learning and proven methods of sound pedagogy.

An understanding of the inherent growth patterns through which children develop as they relate to the creative arts is pertinent to our understanding of the development of creativity at various age levels. Old studies of child development may help us to recognize and understand better those unique conditions which must be set at various age levels as against the general conditions for developing creativity discussed up to this point.

There must be a readiness for creativity just as there is a readiness for reading. Although all children are born with creative drives and creative power, just as all children are born with the potential to love, lack of practice at the psychological time of readiness may impair the function of love—or the function of creativity. Consequently, because of the mistakes of earlier teaching, some children may have to have certain conditions fostered in them before they will be able to create.

Erich Fromm[26] suggests some individual conditions necessary for creative development:

1. The capacity to be puzzled.
2. The ability to concentrate.
3. The ability to experience self.
4. The ability to accept conflict and tension resulting from polarity rather than to avoid them.
5. The willingness to be born everyday.

[25] *Ibid.*, p. 207.

[26] Erich Fromm, "The Creative Attitude" in *Creativity and Its Cultivation*, pp. 44–54.

Each human being is a creation; and as he grows and develops he continues to be a creation in process. His personality is emergent —and the formation of a personality that is creative depends on the experiences he has during the formative periods of that personality.

It is impossible to review all the developmental characteristics and interests of children at each age level in this chapter. It is enough to say that each teacher should frequently review the characteristics, interests and growth patterns of the stages preceding and following the age level of the children with whom she is working, for all children do not grow and develop at the same rate of speed, and a teacher must learn to identify the point of growth and maturation each child has reached. Correct utilization of this knowledge helps the teacher recognize varied abilities in children, and consequently varied stages of creative development.

Creativity has often been destroyed by forcing the child to meet standards which are beyond his abilities. Creative expression changes with the developmental growth of the child. For instance, a new kindergartener is not conscious of the painting he makes and receives little aesthetic enjoyment from it as such, but his creative hunger is being satisfied with the paint itself and this step in his growth gives a type of aesthetic enjoyment necessary for full appreciation later on when he is conscious of the product he paints. The teacher understands that creative efforts on the part of the child may be immature, but this level of immaturity is necessary if the child is to reach a mature stage of development.

In most of the learning processes, children deal first of all with the concrete objects and move gradually into the abstract or symbolic. In creative expression, the opposite *seems* to be true. Children first begin to assemble masses of blocks, or paint with no concrete purpose in mind. These are later identified as garages, houses, or objects which the child has experienced. Later, children communicate freely by use of creative media and reproduce concrete objects recognizable by adults. It would seem, that in the use of some creative materials, the child moves from the abstract to the concrete. A more realistic interpretation might be that he is simply refining the process of creative communication through the use of materials. The initial concrete experience is that with life objects and experiences which he encounters, and the interpretation in art form may be compared to the first attempts to reproduce words by scribbling which later become refined by the technically skilled formation of letters. The mass movements of the little child in using art materials is due to lack of interest or ability to reproduce any specific concrete experience.

As children approach the more sophisticated means of creative expression, they pass through several definite stages of growth. Confronted with art materials of various sorts they must learn to manipulate and to "experiment." This they do best if they are allowed freedom to manipulate to their heart's content. Then comes an exploratory period. At this time they learn what it is like to make bold strokes across a paper with the paint brush. They learn what happens when they scrub the paint on, when they drip it on and when it runs down the page. They have their first experience with texture in paint and paper. They discover the effect of varied sized paint brushes and the effect of the quality of the paint. Proper guidance from the teacher can lead them into explorations with color—they discover what happens when they mix a yellow and a blue, or paint a red over a green.

The young child at this stage of his development is not trying to communicate with art media. He is receiving aesthetic enjoyment from the use of color and materials. His painting at this point is not meant to be anything representative which adults can recognize. This is evidenced by the situation where a young four year old was painting and an interfering adult asked, "What is that supposed to be?" The child looked up, wide-eyed, and said, "How do I know—it's not finished yet!"

It is not long, however, before the child learns to communicate through his painting, his clay, his block construction, his body and his words. This may happen rather suddenly as in the case of a four year old who brought her painting home from school each day and hung it on the wall of her room. One day her father saw it lying on the bed and pinned it on the wall in its usual place. Not long after, he heard an indignant four year old voice exclaim, "Who's dumb, who's awful dumb?"

"What's the matter, Honey?" he asked as he rushed into the bedroom. The four year old stood with her fists planted on her hips, her eyes squinted and her jaw jutting out, looking at the picture.

"Somebody's awful dumb," she said positively, "they hung my picture upside down!!"

When the child discovers he can say things with his materials—

not only to himself but to others as well—he begins to use the language others will understand. His block construction begins to resemble bridges, barns, houses and garages. He has better power of observation and his clay modeling assumes the recognizable form of birds, dogs, rabbits and people. And as his powers of communication through these various media increase, the aesthetic enjoyment the child receives sustains itself or increases also.

This is an important time for guidance of the child. Often the tools the child is using block his method of communication. He cannot manipulate his brush or his crayons to say what he wants to say. Verbalism often fails him at times in oral communication due to lack of background experience and technique, and lack of technique hinders him in artistic expression. Frustration often results, which, if not eliminated by the clever teacher, may cause the child to desert this mode of communication for another over which he has more control. Often, too, the child at this stage resorts to expression through the use of stereotypes. It is essential at this point, then, that the teacher help the child observe, that she lead him to discover new techniques, that she act as a constant guide and inspiration so the child resolves his failures and continues to express himself through various media.

In his adolescent years he becomes more interested in skills and he is more and more critical of his own work. At this stage he has grown from unconscious to conscious creation in his use of all media.

In all of these developmental stages through which the child progresses, his interests and needs will become the subjects for his expression. These interests and needs change with growth changes.

The child's feelings toward the creative process and his attitude toward creative expression are a better evaluation of the teacher's attempts to develop creativity than the paintings he makes, the models he builds, or the poems he writes.

Physical changes help a child acquire new skills and abilities but may create some temporary problems as well. Periods of clumsiness can be overcome readily when tension is absent and the child has ample opportunity to use his changing body in creative ways. Bodily changes are essential to creative expression through movement. When these changes are recognized by the teacher and the child is encouraged to feel proud of his new abilities, embarrassment or ridicule among children over growth changes can be minimized and creative singing, dancing, and dramatization may help the child grow gracefully.

It is important to remember that children must be ready to perform their "developmental tasks." This readiness comes as a result of experience and maturation. The teacher who forces the child into a situation before he is ready is often demanding that the child perform something he is unable to do. The child, confronted by failure and frustration, builds up attitudes and feelings about certain situations which may color his entire life.

SUMMARY

Creativity, as such, cannot be taught. We can only set conditions for it to happen. The task of the elementary school is to set these conditions, which include certain intellectual conditions, proper physical conditions, certain social-emotional conditions, selected psychological conditions and some particular educational conditions.

Creative learning differs from closed-ended, convergent learning in that the outcome is unpredictable. In the creative learning process, there comes a time when the teacher must withdraw from the teaching act and each child must face the unknown by himself.

Palamutlu[27] says that each of the following are aspects of creative teaching: to encourage discovery, to develop the capacity of the child to wonder and to be puzzled, and to stimulate sensitivity. She feels it is the teacher's responsibility to encourage, to give freedom, to swing wide the gates to whatever a child's mind wants to explore, to make contact, to know, to grasp and to stimulate the new to the self. She also states that evaluation should reward creative thinking.

To the College Student

Consider these questions: Which of your college classrooms are more conducive to creative thinking? Why? Do your reasons fall into the same

[27] Neela Palamutlu, "Development of a Manual on Rewarding Creative Thinking in the Early School Years," in *Explorations in Creative Thinking in the Early School Years* (Minneapolis: Bureau of Educational Research, University of Minnesota, 1959), pp. 35–36.

categories mentioned in this chapter? How many ways can you think of to make the time spent in the college classroom a more creative experience?

Do you think you are uncreative? If you feel this way it may be because you have had your own creative attempts suppressed, ridiculed or ignored by others. See how much creativity is left in you. Try some of the following exercises:

- In two minutes list all the uses of a bobby pin you can think of.

- Think of all the answers you can to this question: What would happen if all the plastic in the world should disintegrate?

- Make a list in five minutes of all the ways you might decorate a gymnasium for a dance with only $5 to spend.

Read *The Adventure of Learning in College* by Roger H. Garrison (Harper and Brothers, 1959). Discuss this book from the viewpoint that conditions can be set at the college level to develop creative individuals. Do you believe in this statement?

Hold a debate on the statement, "Creativity cannot be taught; we can only set conditions for it to happen." The bibliography at the end of Chapters I and VIII will provide you with ample material to support your viewpoints.

Most colleges provide for many experiences outside the classrooms where creativity is fostered. To name a few: dances with their various decoration themes; float parades at Spring Weekend; football cheers and band formations; snow sculptures at Winter Carnival time; May Day celebrations, original musicals or stunt nights. Study the conditions under which each of these events becomes possible. What physical conditions are necessary? What tensions are created? Are emotions involved? Where does the thinking for the ideas originate? Who executes them? Are there creative thinkers *and* technicians involved?

There is a good tape recording that will give you ideas about creative teaching. It is published by the Teaching Aids Laboratory, The Ohio State University at Columbus, Ohio. It is by Laura Zirbes, the author of "Spurs to Creative Teaching." Order it this way: No. z-7, *What Creative Teaching Means*, 19 min., $4.50 (cost). Also try No. z-27, *Creative Thinking and Creative Teaching for Creative Living*, two parts, 55 min., $8.00.

To the Classroom Teacher

Consider your own daily program and check it to see if each of the subject matter areas is being utilized to develop the objectives outlined in this chapter.

Keep a record of the times during one day when you were inhibited in your teaching because conditions were not properly set to carry out your ideas. For instance, how many times during the day did scheduling block creative teaching? Lack of proper equipment, lack of necessary paper? Inappropriate room arrangement? What can you do about these factors?

Survey your classroom from an objective point of view. Ask yourself if it seems to belong to the children or if it is predominantly yours? Do their ideas abound or have they been suppressed? Does this simple device help you to evaluate your teaching?

Collect a box of junk—scrap pieces of paper and cloth, pipe cleaners, crepe paper, buttons, glitter, sequins, cupcake papers, wire, milk bottle tops, rubber bands, paper clips, etc. Set aside a time when you allow the children to use these materials. Present them with this problem: *Show me your favorite song by using some of these materials.* See what will happen. Analyze the process as well as the product. Are your children able to solve problems, make decisions and pass judgments creatively? To have some fun, join them. Analyze your own thought processes.

To the College Student and
the Classroom Teacher

Make a collection of articles and books on samples of creative teaching at all levels. They will help you to see how the principles set forth in this chapter can be translated into action.

Examine the atmosphere of the school in which you work. Think of all the rules and regulations which interfere with your creative teaching. Then ask yourself if these rules and regulations really exist or if they are legends of the past, perpetuated by older teachers. How can you find out what you can really do in your classroom?

Check the classroom in which you work against the suggestions in this chapter. Which of these conditions have you fostered—which are neglected?

Re-read the lessons taught in Grade 5, Chapter II and in Grade 1, Chapter IX with these questions in mind:

• Did the teacher set psychological conditions for the experience: was it success-oriented, individuality-oriented, were limits set, did questions evoke confidence and diverse answers, a permissive atmosphere?

• What conditions for developing creativity were not present in these lessons?

• Can all aspects of creativity be developed in *one* lesson or is a series of lessons necessary which concentrates on specific aspects but which eventually develop all?

SELECTED BIBLIOGRAPHY

Association for Childhood Education International, *Children Can Work Independently*. Washington, D. C.: The Association, 1952.

Association for Childhood Education, *Space Arrangement, Beauty in School*. Washington, D. C.: The Association, 1958.

Association for Supervision and Curriculum Development, *Creating a Good Environment for Learning*. Washington, D. C.: National Education Association, 1954.

Beauchamp, G. *Basic Dimensions of Elementary Method*. Boston: Allyn and Bacon, 1959.

Berger, R. M., Guilford, J. P. and Christensen, D. R. "A Factor-Analytic Study of Planning Abilities," *Psychological Monographs*, LXXI, No. 6, 1957.

Biggs, C. "Search for Creativity," *Overview*, II (April 1961), 25–7.

Bryson, L. "Training for Creativity," *School Arts*, LV (Sept. 1960), 5–8.

Christensen, P. R., Guilford, J. P. and Wilson, R. C. "Relations of Creative Responses to Working Time and Instruction," *Journal of Experimental Psychology*, LIII (1957), 82–8.

Cook, P. H. "A Look at Creativity," *School Science Math*, LX (1960), 417–23.

Department of Supervision and Curriculum Development, *Group Planning in Education*. Washington, D. C.: The National Education Association, 1945.

Dunkel, H. B. "Creativity and Education," *Educational Theory*, XI (October 1961), 209–16.

Guilford, J. P. "Factors that Aid and Hinder Creativity," *Teachers College Record*, LXII (February 1962), 380–92.

Hack, Louise E. "Using Committees in the Classroom," *Rinehart Education Pamphlets*. New York: Rinehart and Company, Inc., 1958.

Harap, Henry. *Social Living in the Curriculum*. Nashville, Tennessee: George Peabody College for Teachers, 1952.

Levinger, Leah. "The Teacher's Role in Creativity: Discussion," *American Journal Orthopsychiatry*, XIX (1959), 291–97.

Miel, Alice (ed.). *Creativity in Teaching: Invitations and Instances*. Belmont, California: Wadsworth Publishing Company Inc., 1961.

Myers, R. E. and Torrance, E. P. "Can Teachers Encourage Creative Thinking?" *Educational Leadership*, XIX (1961), 156–59.

Osborn, Alex F. *Applied Imaginations*, rev. ed. New York: Charles Scribner's Sons, 1957.

Stephens, Ada D. *Toward the Development of Creativity in Early Childhood*. University of Toledo: College of Education, 1963.

Strang, Ruth. "Developing Creative Powers of Gifted Children," *Creativity of Gifted and Talented Children*. New York: Bureau of Publications, Teachers College, Columbia University, 1959.

Taylor, Calvin. "Clues to Creative Teaching" (A Series of Ten Articles), *The Instructor* (September-June), 1963–64.

——— (ed.). *The Second University of Utah Research Conference on the Identification of Creative Scientific Talent*. Salt Lake City: University of Utah Press, 1958.

——— (ed.). *Widening Horizons in Creativity*. New York: John Wiley and Sons (in press).

Torrance, E. P. *Creativity: What Research Says to the Teacher*. Washington, D. C.: National Education Association of the United States, 1963.

Wilt, Marion E. *Creativity in the Elementary School*. New York: Appleton-Century-Croft, Inc., 1959.

Wolfson, B. J. "Creativity in the Classroom," *Elementary English*, XXXVIII (November 1961), 523–4.

There is no poetry for the practical man. There is poetry only for the mankind of the man who spends a certain amount of his life turning the mechanical wheel. But let him spend too much of his life at the mechanics of practicality and either he must become something less of a man, or his very mechanical efficiency will become impaired by the frustrations stored up in his irrational human personality. An ulcer, gentlemen, is an unkissed imagination taking its revenge for having been jilted. It is an unwritten poem, a neglected music, an unpainted water color, an undanced dance. It is a declaration from the mankind of the man that a clear spring of joy has not been tapped, and that it must break through, muddily, on its own.[1]

—JOHN CIARDI

[1] John Ciardi, from a speech entitled, "An Ulcer, Gentlemen, Is an Unwritten Poem," 1955-56.

IX——Principles Basic
to Creative Teaching

FOLLOWING is a "contrived" experience planned for a slow first grade class in a culturally deprived area. It is built around the teaching of the language arts. The teacher (a demonstration teacher) used a current, popular holiday as the theme of the lesson: Valentine's Day. It is a good example of a creative language arts situation.

The teacher's objectives were as follows:

(1) To develop an oral and written vocabulary among the children especially one pertaining to Valentine's Day.

(2) To develop some creative writing among the children.

(3) To develop some meaningful reading material among the children.

(4) To develop some good listening skills.

(5) To develop good oral expression through the use of choral speaking.

The experience was planned to last an entire afternoon. Notice how the teacher had set conditions to insure the success of his work.

The teacher proceeded by passing out white hearts on which the children printed their names. These became nametags which each child pinned on. Because the teacher was not the regular teacher, he talked awhile with the children to establish rapport and to explain why he was spending the afternoon with them. Each child spoke his name and the teacher also wore a name tag.

The lesson then proceeded as follows:

"Who can tell me what holiday is coming up next week?" asked the teacher.

"Valentine's Day," the children chorused.

"That's right!" the teacher said, "and I want to tell you a story about Valentine's Day and something that happened to me. It's a sad story and I may need you to help me tell it."

Here the teacher is providing motivation and encouraging involvement of all the children.

"Well, it seems," the teacher went on, "that a group of boys and girls were in my office yesterday making valentines for a party. All day long they made valentines, and finally, around dinner time, they cleaned up the room and went home. Now when I went into my office this morning, I noticed something that made me feel quite sad. It was a valentine that hadn't been finished. I brought it along."

Here the teacher brought out from behind the desk a huge piece of poster board on which there was drawn a large red heart.

"How do you think you would feel if you were a valentine and Valentine's Day was coming up soon, and you weren't finished?"

The words came fluently—the teacher here was using simple divergent thinking processes through association. All answers were accepted and printed on a sheet of primary paper. Such words as sad, lonely, awful, lonesome, unhappy, crying, miserable, badly, sick, uncomfortable and many others appeared on the chart.

"Yes, I guess maybe we would feel all of those things," said the teacher, "and I have written them down so we won't forget them and may use them a little later on. Well, I'm going to use a few of them right now to tell you more of the story. I'm going to use the words sad and lonely, and call my story, 'The Sad, Lonely Valentine That Didn't Get Finished.' What do you think we could do to make the valentine feel happy?"

"Finish it," exclaimed one child.

"A good idea," said the teacher. "Let's do just that—and I'll let you help me tell the story. First of all we'll need to think of some things we might put on valentines to make them pretty. You think of all the things you can and I will print the words up here where all can see and where we will not forget them."

Soon a long list appeared on the primary chart paper: hearts, arrows, cupids, angels, bows, ribbon, lace, doilies, gold, red, flowers, lovers, pictures, colored paper, crepe paper, etc.

"Well," said the teacher, "those are all good ideas and I just happen to have something here that will help us to finish our story." Here the teacher brought out a decorated valentine box. The children exclaimed in awe. One was asked to read what it said on the top. He read, "Box for Making Valentines." The children then guessed what might be in it.

Soon it was opened and the teacher took out a collection of materials he had gathered for decorating the valentine. When the word describing the object was already on the chart, the object was held against the word; when it was not the word was added. The box contained bows, rosebuds, paper lace, gold doilies, ribbon, crepe paper, silhouettes, etc. Each child was allowed to choose something that he liked from the box. When all had their own object, the teacher gave each a little ball of adhesive putty so they could fasten it to the valentine.

"Now, let's get on with our story," said the teacher. "I am going to ask you to play act it with me. From now on I am the sad, lonely valentine that never was finished." The teacher then held the cardboard with the heart on it so just his head showed over the top.

"I'm a sad, lonely, miserable, unhappy valentine," the teacher said. "Yesterday when some boys and girls were making valentines they forgot to finish me, and I will never belong to anyone if I look like this. But look at all these boys and girls—maybe they could help me out—they look like nice boys and girls. Allen, I'm a sad, lonely valentine looking for someone to finish me for Valentine's Day. Do you think you could help me?"

Allen immediately rose to the occasion. "Yes," he said, "I've got a rosebud I could put on you."

"Oh, you are so kind," said the valentine. "Would you put it on me somewhere please?"

Allen stuck the rosebud on to the valentine.

"Oh," said the valentine, "I feel better already. Thank you, Allen."

"You're welcome," said Allen.

"Here's a little girl over here who looks like she might help me," said the valentine. "Emmy, I'm a sad, lonely valentine looking for someone to decorate me. Could you help me?"

"Yes, I could," said Emmy, "I have a big pink bow." And she stuck it on the valentine.

The teacher went from child to child carrying on a conversation with each and working a variety of responses. It is interesting to note how he developed spontaneity with this technique. Finally he surrendered the valentine to Allen and Allen became the valentine going from child to child until all the children had had a chance to decorate the valentine.

"Let's find an ending to the story," said the teacher after Allen had visited the last child.

Ideas came one by one and the teacher helped put them together.

"So the sad, lonely valentine was soon decorated by all the boys and girls. He was decorated with arrows, hearts, lace, gold doilies, ribbons, bows and silhouettes. Now he was ready for Valentine's Day, so he wasn't sad any more."

"Wasn't that fun?" said the teacher. "And our valentine certainly is beautiful," he added as he printed the word beautiful on chart paper. "Beautiful is a good word that tells about the valentine. Can you think of any other words that tell about our valentine? I will print them here so we won't forget them and can use them later."

Soon the following words appeared on the primary paper: wonderful, lovely, lacy, gorgeous, colorful, happy, bright, gay, delightful, big, huge, red, pink and white, gold-lacy, alive, pink-pretty.

"Those are excellent words," said the teacher. "Now I'd like to tell you about something that we forgot. Do you have any idea what it is?"

They could not guess so the teacher opened the large valentine to disclose two empty sheets inside. "What does it need to be really finished?" asked the teacher.

"A poem," they chorused.

"Yes, let's write a poem to go inside," said Emmy.

"All right," said the teacher. "Here is some paper. If you want to write one of your own go ahead, and those who don't, can write one with me. Who has some ideas?" They decided to make it rhyme and not rhyme. Rhyming was discussed. Then ideas began to come.

> Once there was a valentine
> Miserable and sad
> We decorated him
> To make him glad
>
> Allen put on a gorgeous rose
> Emmy put on a soft bow
> Mary put on beautiful lace
> Joey put on a pink ribbon
>
> Hal put on a romantic cupid
> Susan pasted frilly crepe paper
> Patty had a sharp arrow
> John cracked the red heart

At this point the demonstration teacher asked the regular teacher to leave the room. As soon as the regular teacher was gone, the demonstration teacher said, "I have a good idea. Why don't we finish our poem so we can give it to Mrs. Murdock for a Valentine? Do you like that idea?"

The children were remotivated to the point where they added this verse to their "poem":

> Now he's all ready
> For Valentine's Day
> And so with our love
> We give him away.

"Can you think of any way we might say our poem to Mrs. Murdock when she comes in?" asked the teacher.

The children discussed many ideas. They decided that the teacher would print the poem inside the Valentine and they would all read it when Mrs. Murdock returned to the room.

"We *could* make a talking valentine," said the teacher, "by putting the poem on the tape recorder."

They were excited about this and discussed ways they might do it. Immediately one was chosen and they tried it out by practicing it once. When they had finished Joanna suggested it sounded a little flat and said, "Why don't we all shout, 'Happy Valentine's Day, Mrs. Murdock' at the end?" The poem was taped with gratifying results. The nametags were then decorated and stuck around the poem on the inside of the valentine so each child's name appeared there. Then two boys volunteered to hold the Valentine and to present it to Mrs. Murdock. Another was chosen to run the tape and another to fetch Mrs. Murdock.

Bruno brought Mrs. Murdock into the room and sat her in a chair in the front of the room. He said, "Mrs. Murdock, we have a surprise for you. We have a singing valentine!" Allen and James came forth with the valentine and opened it. Sally pushed the button to play the tape. Mrs. Murdock was properly surprised and pleased. The children hugged themselves and giggled with self satisfaction.

Because the afternoon was nearly over, the teacher said, "I'll leave all these wonderful words here and maybe tomorrow you can write me stories and poems using these words."

Several were written; one especially effective one was:

> Red, pink
> Hearts, roses
> I love you!
> Soft, lacy
> Valentines
> I love you!
> Love is wonderful
> Valentines say it
> I love you!

That this experience obtained creative responses in the children is obvious. A summary list of the basic principles of creative teaching, culled from research, will help to show how this lesson was creative and will help to point up the contrasts in creative and non-creative teaching.

Principles of Creative Teaching

1. *IN CREATIVE TEACHING, SOMETHING NEW, DIF-FERENT OR UNIQUE RESULTS:* In this lesson, there were new ideas, a new poem, a new dramatization, a new story, a new way of saying it into the tape, new individual poems, new word lists. The children tapped their own unique experiences, shared them with the group and came up with some new group and individual experiences.

2. *IN CREATIVE TEACHING, DIVERGENT THINK-ING PROCESSES ARE STRESSED:* Nowhere, after the first question in the lesson, was any *specific* answer called for. Known facts and words were constantly being used in new experiences—no one way of doing anything was required; all ways were heard and the most fitting one accepted and applied.

3. *IN CREATIVE TEACHING, MOTIVATIONAL TEN-SIONS ARE A PREREQUISITE TO THE CREATIVE PROC-ESS. THE PROCESS SERVES AS A TENSION-RELIEVING AGENT:* Robertson, the composer, felt that one characteristic of the ideal teacher was to think and perform creatively in the classroom and thus stimulate surprise and curiosity. In this lesson, the teacher provided high-tension motivations and re-motivations but did not feel "bound" to stick to any one. He could have shifted from one motivation to another had the proper tensions not been produced.

4. *IN CREATIVE TEACHING, OPEN-ENDED SITUA-TIONS ARE UTILIZED:* Once psychological security had been established so children understood materials and processes, the teacher left the learning to the children to take where they would. One idea sparked another. Open-endedness was particularly notice-able in presenting the dramatization, in using the decorations on the valentine, in suggesting "something"· should go inside, in determining how to put the poem on tape, in determining how to present the valentine to Mrs. Murdock and in setting the stage for individual creative writing.

[157]

5. *IN CREATIVE TEACHING, THERE COMES A TIME WHEN THE TEACHER WITHDRAWS AND CHILDREN FACE THE UNKNOWN THEMSELVES:* Notice how the teacher withdrew from the dramatization and allowed the children to go forward on their own. These children also faced a void which they filled when they composed the poem, when they found ways to make the valentine "talk" effectively and when they wrote their own poems.

6. *IN CREATIVE TEACHING, THE OUTCOMES ARE UNPREDICTABLE:* The teacher in this experience obviously hoped the tensions he built would lead to some particular objectives. But the specific outcomes he could not predict. The unpredictable outcomes of the experience were: (1) the way the story-dramatization worked out; (2) the poem written for the inside of the valentine; (3) the manner of taping it; and (4) the way the children would use the words on the chart and other words in their individual writing.

7. *IN CREATIVE TEACHING, CONDITIONS ARE SET WHICH MAKE POSSIBLE PRECONSCIOUS THINKING:* This principle encourages children to draw from all of life's experiences and to give expression to them. This is where Rugg would feel that we should make it possible for children to draw from the whole life continuum by keeping their minds in the transliminal chamber.

Notice in the lesson above how the teacher encouraged associations with preconscious thinking: "What can we use to decorate a valentine? How would you feel if you were an unfinished valentine?" and the complete acceptance of all the ideas the children presented.

8. *CREATIVE TEACHING MEANS THAT STUDENTS ARE ENCOURAGED TO GENERATE AND DEVELOP THEIR OWN IDEAS:* We might use other lessons I have observed or taught to demonstrate some of these points and show a contrast in uncreative and creative approaches to teaching.

Miss Henry, in the sixth grade, gave her children a list of twenty new, unusual words to look up in the dictionary and copy their definitions.

Miss Lomax, on the other hand, knew that vocabulary develops best when the words come from the listening and oral experiences of boys and girls. She had the children collect words they heard at the shopping center, on the school bus, on TV, at the movies, in school. If they did not understand a new word or an old one put to new uses, they entered it on a word chart hanging in the sixth grade room. Once a week they spent time discussing these new words and using them to build more picturesque and creative speech. After a particularly exciting discussion of the various meanings of the word "quiet," and how it can have physical, emotional and social values, one sixth grade boy wrote:

WHAT IS QUIET?

Quiet is the silent hills
  Quiet is the baby's sleep
Quiet is the lake so calm
  And the river running deep.

Quiet is the silent night
  And the people bowed in prayer;
Quiet is the candlelight
  Quiet stands for loving care.

Quiet is the icy snow.
  Quiet is the newborn spring.
Quiet is the sunlight's glow;
  Quiet is a precious thing!

9. *IN CREATIVE TEACHING, DIFFERENCES, UNIQUENESS, INDIVIDUALITY, ORIGINALITY ARE STRESSED AND REWARDED:* In one kindergarten Miss Lomax played cowboy music and showed all the children how to respond rhythmically. Soon all 25 children were shuffling along and winding up to toss a lasso.

In another kindergarten, Miss Ellis played cowboy music and asked any one child to interpret it through bodily rhythms. Then she asked for another interpretation, then another and another. Soon she had 25 *different* interpretations of cowboy rhythms.

10. *IN CREATIVE TEACHING, THE PROCESS IS AS IMPORTANT AS THE PRODUCT:* In the valentine experience narrated above, the children followed the steps of creative production over and over again. Although the narration does not tell how the children experienced the process, the teacher was able to observe that the children were creating: first there was the warm-up period of preparation as the teacher built tensions because he knew the developmental needs and interests of children of this age level. Involvement was obvious in the way the children entered the spirit of the dramatization, in writing the poem, in making the tape and in writing individual poems even after the lesson was over. Incubation periods were short—but all the children were thinking, and hands would wave as an insight or a new idea came. The period of illumination was obvious when the valentine was completed, when the poem was satisfactory to all, when the tape was completed. The evaluation period came in polishing up the presentation for Mrs. Murdock. While all steps of the process were not as detailed or as prolonged as they might always appear in the act of creating, on this grade level and with these slow children they were still obviously apparent.

11. *IN CREATIVE TEACHING CERTAIN CONDITIONS MUST BE SET TO PERMIT CREATIVITY TO APPEAR:* The valentine experience fulfilled many of the conditions mentioned in Chapter VIII. Physical conditions were such that the chair arrangement made possible the little dramatization, the use of the chalkboard and the chart papers, and the making of the tape. The teacher set conditions for good rapport with the students, and built successfully that coveted "air of expectancy." Certain psychological securities were established: all ideas were accepted and all children were encouraged to give ideas; all children were involved; a base vocabulary was created to give all children something to fall back on and to operate from; good social rapport was built with the teacher respecting each child's contribution; no child experienced failure; the teacher kept goading the children on by encouraging modification, substitution, additions and new modes of expression. Intellectual conditions abounded in the challenge for creative thinking, in the problems posed, in the teasing of the imagination; former knowledge and skills were drawn on and put to new uses, divergent thinking processes were utilized and ques-

tions and discussion were so planned that fluency of ideas and individuality were rewarded.

12. *IN CREATIVE TEACHING, TEACHING IS "SUCCESS" RATHER THAN "FAILURE" ORIENTED:*   In the valentine experience no child failed. Failure may lead to creative thinking but when the teacher uses failure experiences as a base for creative production, they are no longer failures—they have been turned into successes.

13. *IN CREATIVE TEACHING, PROVISION IS MADE TO LEARN KNOWLEDGE AND SKILLS BUT PROVISION IS ALSO MADE TO APPLY THESE IN NEW PROBLEM-SOLVING SITUATIONS:*   In a sixth grade class the need for a 3-dimensional map arose and Mr. Arnold, the teacher, said he would show the class how to make one. Without bothering to find out what the children knew about making 3-dimensional maps, he showed them how to make a salt and flour map.

Mr. Endres, on the other hand, had the children list all the materials they knew could be used 3-dimensionally. From these the children chose those which best fitted their criteria for the map. *They* decided on salt and flour because it held its shape, could be painted, was light and could be transported easily about the room, could be hung and was easy to work with. All these children were putting old experiences into new patterns: they were using many "divergent" answers to problems, were evaluating, passing judgment and developing the affiliated skills of creative production.

14. *IN CREATIVE TEACHING, SELF-INITIATED LEARNING IS ENCOURAGED:*   Examples of this are evident in the valentine experience. "Finish it!" one little girl exclaimed when asked what to do to make the valentine happy. "A poem!" shouted a child when asked what to put inside. The invention of word-combinations such as "gold-lacy" and "pink-pretty" shows self-initiated learning.

15. *IN CREATIVE TEACHING, SKILLS OF CONSTRUCTIVE CRITICISM AND EVALUATION SKILLS ARE DEVELOPED:*   Although constructive criticism and self-evaluation are not as apparent at this grade level as at some of the older levels,

we still see evidences of it in Joanna's remarking that the poem sounded flat and her suggesting that the class shout "Happy Valentine's Day, Mrs. Murdock!" at the end of the tape.

Constructive criticism was well-employed in Mr. Enders' class when the children applied the necessary criteria to the final construction of the map.

16. *IN CREATIVE TEACHING, IDEAS AND OBJECTS ARE MANIPULATED AND EXPLORED:* In the valentine experience, the children manipulated and explored word-combinations, voice-combinations, paper, flo-pens, lace doilies, gold doilies, artificial flowers, construction paper, crepe paper, poster paper, putty, glue, ideas, machines and each other.

17. *CREATIVE TEACHING EMPLOYS DEMOCRATIC PROCESSES:* In all the samples of creative teaching in this chapter, the children take part in planning the work, and are responsible for creative output. The teacher is not authoritarian but he guides, suggests, helps and sets realistic limits.

18. *IN CREATIVE TEACHING, METHODS ARE USED WHICH ARE UNIQUE TO THE DEVELOPMENT OF CREATIVITY:* This principle will be discussed in the following paragraphs.

Unique Methods for Developing Creativity

It will be a delightful day when the creative powers of children are developed from birth, and practice in creative problem-solving and creative production are an accepted part of the school program. But, since that condition does not currently exist, and since much of the creative teaching of the present is an attempt to make up for faulty teaching of the past, teachers today need to be concerned with the reconstruction of the creative powers of the children currently enrolled in our elementary schools. We need to examine then, those studies and reports which have been concerned with recapturing and developing the creative process in children and adults. Some current experimentation has revealed unique techniques which develop creativity.

The Minnesota Studies[2] contributed some specific ideas for required conditions to promote creativity. These researchers found, for instance, that too frequent use of evaluation during practice sessions of creative writing, regardless of type, seemed to interfere with subsequent performance on similar tasks. Unevaluated ("off the record") practice tends to produce greater originality, elaboration, and sensitivity than evaluated practice in most instances, except at the sixth grade levels. When peer evaluation was used, creative evaluation (constructive) rather than critical (destructive) tended to be more effective in producing originality, elaboration, sensitivity, except in kindergarten through the third grade.

In the Department of Creative Education at the University of Buffalo each summer, Dr. Sidney Parnes runs a workshop for the purpose of developing the creative powers of people from all lines of work. Dr. Parnes' course has been printed and is available for interested parties to use.[3]

Dr. Parnes' course is based on much of the work of Dr. Alex Osborn,[4] one of the pioneers of the creative movement. His research on the value of his course to the development of creativity in humans is very gratifying. He has come to believe that people can be made more creative in their thinking through the conscientious development of those areas of the intellect which stimulate divergent thinking processes. Since other researchers have not been as successful as Dr. Parnes a review of his work is important here. Dr. Parnes stresses the following factors as blocks to creativity:

(1) *Lack of knowledge:* here creativity is more easily developed if a large number of elements relating to a problem are known. All our senses should be put to work absorbing knowledge and then knowledge should be put to work for us.

(2) *Habit:* thinking in terms of previous solutions to problems, or along accepted lines tends to limit our imagination. We become hide-bound and uncreative through habit.

---

[2] E. P. Torrance, "Education and Creativity" in Taylor, Calvin W., *Creativity: Progress and Potential* (New York: McGraw-Hill), pp. 103–6.

[3] Sidney J. Parnes, *Student Workbook for Creative Problem-Solving Courses and Institutes* (Rev. ed.; Buffalo: State University of New York Book Store, 1963).

[4] Alex F. Osborn, *Applied Imagination* (3rd rev. ed.; New York: Charles Scribner's Sons, 1963).

(3) *Attitudinal Blocks:* these are "sets" we have in our minds that close them to imaginative thinking. Among common attitudinal blocks are lack of a positive outlook, conformity, reliance on authority, and lack of effort towards positive thinking or problem-solving.

In Dr. Parnes' course, individual ideation and group ideation are developed. Brainstorming as a technique for producing new and original ideas also proves to be effective (see Volume IV). Parnes[5] points out that creative evaluation can be different from other types of assessment. Ideas produced during creative ideation periods should be treated as "diamonds in the rough." They may not be worth much in their initial form but may be developed into valuable ideas if creatively processed.

Scientific research at the State University at Buffalo has found that students consistently produce substantially more good ideas when they follow the *principle of deferred judgment* than when they allow their judgment concurrently to interfere with their idea-finding.[6]

Deferred judgment does not mean that evaluation is ignored, however; it is "put off" until all ideas are out. It gives the individual or the group more ideas to which to apply the evaluative criteria. Individuals are less apt to reject ideas or apply preconceived limitations or criteria if they look at the idea and *evaluate* it than they do if they refuse to examine an idea in the first place. But, eventually, evaluation is essential to the creative process. A good example of the use of deferred judgment was given on page 55 in the illustration of the students planning for the Junior Prom. In the experience narrated at the beginning of this Chapter, the teacher used deferred judgment in many instances: (1) *many* possible words were listed before best ones were chosen; (2) *many* possible ideas for the choral poem were given before one was chosen; (3) *many* suggestions for valentine decorations were listed before the children chose one, etc.

In Alex Osborn's book *Applied Imagination*[7], many illustra-

[5] Sidney J. Parnes, *Instructor's Manual for Semester Courses in Creative Problem-Solving* (Rev. ed.; Buffalo: Creative Education Foundation, 1963), p. 33.

[6] *Ibid.*, p. 43.

[7] Osborn, *op. cit.*, pp. 69-327.

tions are given to help people *stretch* their ability to produce creative ideas. Osborn has the creator ask himself these questions to stretch and expand his creative thinking:

(1) To what *new uses* can it be put?

(2) How can I *adapt* the idea to another use? What else is like this? What other ideas does it suggest?

(3) How can I *modify* the idea? For instance, could I change the meaning, color, motion, sound, odor, taste, form, shape—give it a new twist?

(4) How could I *magnify* the idea? Could I add something to it—more time, greater frequency, extra value—make it stronger, higher, longer, thicker, larger, heavier? Could I duplicate, multiply, exaggerate?

(5) Could I *minify* the idea: subtract something, make smaller, condense, put in miniature, lower, shorten, narrow, lighten, omit, slow, streamline, understate?

(6) Could I *substitute:* who else, what else, other ingredients, other material, other process, other place, other power, other plane, other approach, other tone of voice, other time?

(7) Could I *rearrange* it: change components, pattern, layout, sequence, schedule, change pace?

(8) Could I *reverse* it: transpose positive and negative, opposites, turn it around, turn it backward, upside down, inside out, reverse roles, turn tables, transfer cause and effect?

(9) Could I *combine* it with something else: a blend, an alloy, an assortment, an ensemble, combine units, purposes, appeals, ideas?

Parnes has devised a workbook where exercises in creative idea-stretching are developed by the application of Osborn's idea-spurring questions.[8]

Parnes also tells of some other techniques which can be used to develop creative output.

One such idea is *attribute-listing*.[9] This is in essence a kind of checklist procedure. Developed by Professor Robert P. Crawford, this technique requires the problem-solver to list the various attributes of an object or idea. Then he turns his attention specifically

[8] Parnes, *Student Workbook*, p. 52.

[9] Parnes, *Instructor's Manual*, p. 52.

to each one of these attributes. In focusing on each attribute, the creator thinks of ideas to improve it—applying Osborn's idea-spurring questions.

Another idea is the *forced-relationships technique*.[10] This is the technique which calls for a forced relationship between two or more normally unrelated products or ideas as a starting point for the idea-generation process. For example, in thinking of a desk and a chair separately, the creator might combine them then into a desk with a recessed chair, a folding desk and chair combination, a portable desk and chair combination.

Parnes also uses the technique of *morphological analysis*. This pertains to the structure of things: hence, morphological analysis deals with an analysis of structure. Once the structure is analyzed, forced-relationship techniques are used, so as quickly to produce countless idea possibilities.[11]

Among the attributes of creative people is their greater sensitivity to problems. Dr. Parnes hopes to build in students as a result of his course an attitude of "constructive discontent." This, he feels, should help them become more sensitive to the problems around them.

There are three types of questions: (1) fact finding questions, (2) decision or judgment questions and (3) creative questions. The first two types call for facts or judgment; the third type calls for ideas. Such a question as, "How can I make fractions interesting to my fifth grade?" is one. While all questions involve some fact-finding, only the third requires new ideas. "Facts become springboards for the imagination" says Dr. Parnes. Much creative thinking can be induced when questions calling for ideas are asked or when fact-finding questions are answered and then facts are put to work in new patterns or ideas.

Another aid to creative thinking is a careful definition of the problem, or a redefinition of any given problem. Defining and re-defining a problem helps the individual to visualize more than one mode of attack. A new viewpoint may often open the way to a solution.

Narrowing a broad problem into specific problems or sub-problems helps the individual focus on creative ways of attacking

10 *Ibid.*, p. 54.
11 *Ibid.*, p. 56.

the sub-problems, which in turn will bring a creative solution to the whole problem. A problem such as, "How can we raise money for our senior trip to Washington?" may be broken down into many sub-problems such as, "What can we *make* to sell at a profit? What affairs can we give for *entertainment* that will provide us with a profit? What *services* can we provide that will realize a profit?" Brainstorming each of the sub-problems eventually leads to the solution of the large problem.

From the work of Dr. Parnes, Dr. Osborn, Dr. Torrance and others, then, the last basic principle on page 162 may be justifiably added to the list of basic principles. It is repeated below:

IN CREATIVE TEACHING THERE ARE METHODS WHICH ARE UNIQUE TO THE DEVELOPMENT OF CREATIVITY.

In summary, these special methods include the following:

1. APPLICATION OF THE PRINCIPLE OF DEFERRED JUDGMENT.

2. REMOVAL OF KNOWN BLOCKS TO CREATIVITY.

3. BRAINSTORMING.

4. CREATIVE EVALUATION.

5. EXPANDING CREATIVE THINKING AND CREATIVE PRODUCTION THROUGH QUESTIONS STRESSING NEW USES, ADAPTATION, MODIFICATION, MAGNIFICATION, MINIFICATION, SUBSTITUTION, REARRANGEMENT.

6. APPLICATION OF THE TECHNIQUE OF ATTRIBUTE-LISTING, FORCED RELATIONSHIPS, AND MORPHOLOGICAL ANALYSIS.

7. HELPING PEOPLE BECOME MORE SENSITIVE TO PROBLEMS.

8. A CAREFUL STATING OR DEFINITION OF A PROBLEM.

9. NARROWING A BROAD PROBLEM INTO SPECIFIC SUB-PROBLEMS.

10. ALLOWING A PROBLEM TO "INCUBATE" FOR A PERIOD OF TIME.

These, then, are the basic principles from which creative teaching rises. Teachers must recognize and utilize these principles in planning work with the children if creativity is to be developed. No one lesson can include all these principles any more than any *one* lesson in reading develops all reading skills. But a series of lessons must be planned which will employ all of these techniques, and these lessons must be everyday occurrences rather than occasional spectacles. As much attention should be given to the application of these particular principles to teaching as is currently given to other known principles of learning. New principles for developing creativity may be added as time advances and research progresses. But we do not need to wait any longer—a conscientious effort to apply these already known and tried basic principles and techniques could go a long way in promoting the creative development of every boy and girl in our classrooms today.

SUMMARY

Creative teaching is a method of teaching which differs dramatically from the traditional approaches to teaching. Its principles have been stated in this chapter.

Educational programs in the future will be governed by these basic principles:

(1) the development of creative power is a major objective of the school; (2) children are taught to use problem-solving processes; (3) teachers capitalize on the creative drives of children whenever possible; (4) teaching is directed to the development of divergent thinking processes as well as convergent; (5) "open-ended" learning situations are employed; (6) children are made more sensitive to environmental stimuli; (7) differences between "creative" and "critical" thinking are recognized and teaching is directed to develop both; (8) a tolerance is developed for new ideas; (9) children are not subjected to blind or meaningless conformity and rigidity; (10) democratic procedures are practiced in the classroom; (11) the steps in the creative process are recognized, and "polished" products are not expected at the onset of the creative experience; (12) all areas of the curriculum are regarded as instruments to develop creativity; (13) provision is made for learning many facts and skills, but provision is also made for children to use these facts and skills in new, ongoing situations; (14) self-initiated learning is encouraged and evaluated; (15) skills of constructive criticism are developed; (16) evaluation skills are taught and practiced; and (17) teaching is "success" rather than "failure" oriented.

It is significant to note that all research in creativity up to this point has been of conditions as they currently exist—when very little planned, organized teaching is done FOR creativity. Creative teachers, up to this time, have been creative because of their sensitivity to children, their flair for novelty and originality, their unique ability to communicate, and their sense of values regarding differences in children. When present knowledge about developing creativity is translated into practical application in the classrooms, the results of similar research should be vastly different.

To the College Student

Let yourself go. Using John Ciardi's quotation at the beginning of this chapter, write as many definitions of an ulcer as you can. Be poetic! Be uninhibited! Be original!

At the beginning of this chapter is a "contrived" experience where basic principles of creativity were applied to a slow-learning group of children on a low primary level. Now devise a "natural" experience which uses as many of the basic principles as possible.

Divide your class into small groups. Assign one of the basic principles of creative teaching as presented in this chapter to each group and have the members of the group plan a "natural" or "contrived" lesson in any area of the curriculum which develops their basic principle. Share your ideas.

Ask your librarian to obtain the pamphlet *Creativity and College Teaching* (Bulletin of the Bureau of School Service: College of Education, University of Kentucky, Vol. XXXV, No. 4 June 1963). Read it and discuss ways college classes may be conducted to develop the basic principles of creativity.

Select from your own experiences in elementary school, or from more recent observation, those lessons which you feel were particularly non-creative and those which were creative. Discuss these ideas to discover which of the principles stated in this chapter were present or absent.

To the Classroom Teacher

Make a check list of the principles basic to creative teaching as they are listed in this chapter. At the end of each school day for one week, check off those principles which you have used to plan your classroom teaching. At the end of the week note how many of them guided your own teaching. Could such a checklist provide an evaluation of the creativeness of teaching?

What sort of discussion and teaching do you think preceded the writing of the poem, "What Is Quiet" on page 159? Could you reconstruct this lesson in your mind?

This chapter points out that teachers can begin to expand the creative powers of their children at once. Here are some ideas to try out on your students:

- List *all* the uses you can think of for an old magazine (principle of ideation: new uses).

- List all the meanings that come to your mind for the word "blue" (principle of ideation: adaptiveness).

- Here is a situation. How could we solve it?

    A tractor truck was going under a covered bridge when the top of it hit the bottom of the bridge. The driver stopped and noted that all he needed was 2 inches to get his load under the bridge. List all the ways you can think of to get the truck under the bridge. Then apply these criteria to determine which idea is best (principle of modification and evaluation):

    Which idea is most practical?
    Which will be least time-consuming?
    Which will cause the least damage?
    Which will cause the smallest traffic tie-up?
    Which will be the least expensive?

- Place 2 funnels, a candle and some colored paper on a table before the class and discuss all the things that could be made from them (principle of rearrangement).

- Place a pretty glass before the class. Ask "What can I add to this glass so I could use it for many things?" (principles of magnification and combination).

Think of many ideas you can use with your children to develop the ideation principles mentioned on pages 164-167.

Ask your children this question, "If there were a fire in the school building, how could we still have school?" and write down all the ideas which come in the following five minutes. Then give them this question for homework: "If we had no books, how could we learn about things going on in the world?" Permit them to have 24 hours for an incubation period, then ask them for their ideas. Did the incubation period produce *more* ideas? More creative ones? More logical ones?

To the College Student and the Classroom Teacher

Miss Jones is an art teacher. Twice a week she visits every grade in the Centerville school system for 20 minutes each. Miss Jones enters the room exactly at the time she is supposed to enter. She expects each teacher to have all the children ready: feet on floor, desks cleared, eyes ahead, mouths closed. Miss Jones wheels in a cart of art materials which she has carefully prepared the previous evening. When she enters each room she takes over. Her philosophy is that the art instruction of the children of the district is her job and no non-professionals should meddle with her work. As soon as the art lesson is under way, the regular teacher leaves the classroom. Miss Jones likes it that way.

In light of our discussion of creativity, discuss these two questions: Is the art program fulfilling its purpose? Is Miss Jones a creative person?

What would be a better plan for the use of the art consultant than the one described above?

There is a booklet you will enjoy called *Toward The Development of Creativity in Early Childhood* (Stephens, Ada D. (ed.), *Educational Comment*. Toledo: College of Education, 1963). This booklet gives illustrations of how each area of the elementary school curriculum may be used to develop creativity. Read it with the purpose of noting how the principles described in this chapter are used to develop creativity through a variety of media.

Creative teaching is "success" oriented. Does this mean that children should never have failure experiences? Is there a difference between "failure" and a "failure experience?"

SELECTED BIBLIOGRAPHY

Anderson, Harold H. (ed.). *Creativity and its Cultivation*. New York: Harper and Brothers, 1959.

Armstrong, F. A. *Idea-Tracking*. New York: Criterion Books, 1960.

Barkan, Manuel and Mooney, Ross L. (eds.). *The Conference on Creativity: A Report to the Rockefeller Foundation.* Columbus, Ohio: Ohio State University Press, 1953.

Barron, F. "The Disposition Toward Originality," *Journal of Abnormal and Social Psychology,* LI, No. 3 (1955), 478–85.

Biber, B. "Premature Structuring as a Deterrant to Creativity," *American Journal of Orthopsychiatry,* 29 (1959), 280–90.

Clark, C. H. *Brainstorming.* Garden City: Doubleday and Company, 1958.

Ghiselin, B. *The Creative Process.* New York: Mentor Books, 1955.

Lehner, George F. J. and Kube, Ella. *The Dynamics of Personal Adjustment.* Englewood Cliffs, N. J.: Prentice-Hall Inc., 1955.

Lowenfeld, V. *Creative and Mental Growth.* New York: MacMillan Co. (rev. ed.), 1952.

Maslow, A. H. "Cognition of Being in the Peak-experiences," *Journal of Genetic Psychology,* XCIV (March 1959), 43–66.

Mearns, Hughes. *Creative Power: The Education of Youth in the Creative Arts* (rev. ed.). New York: Dover Publications, 1929.

Miel, Alice (ed.). *Creativity in Teaching: Invitations and Instances.* Belmont, California: Wadsworth Publishing Company, Inc., 1961.

Moustakas, Clark. *The Self.* New York: Harper and Row, 1956.

Murphy, Gardner. *Human Potentialities.* New York: Basic Books, Inc., 1958.

Patrick, Catherine. *What Is Creative Thinking?* New York: Philosophical Library, 1955.

Russel, David E. *Children's Thinking.* New York: Ginn and Co., 1956.

Smith, Paul (ed.). *An Examination of the Creative Process.* New York: Publishers Inc., 1959.

Stein, Morris I. and Heinze, Shirley. *Creativity and the Individual.* Glencoe, Illinois: The Free Press, 1960.

Torrance, E. P. "Current Research on the Nature of Creative Talent," *Journal of Counseling Psychology,* VI, No. 4 (1959), 309–16.

Whiting, C. S. *Creative Thinking.* New York: Reinhold, 1958.

Williams, F. E. *Foundations of Creative Problem Solving.* Ann Arbor: Edwards Bros., 1960.

*I*magination is more important than knowledge.

———————————————————————————————Albert Einstein

X——The Role of Creativity
in the Elementary
School Curriculum

CREATIVITY was once considered a "garnish" or a "frill" to the basic elementary school curriculum. Currently we have come to regard it more as the very core of the total curriculum itself; the basis for learning and self-realization. As the core of learning, curriculum planning and teaching methodology, it assumes a role of major importance in each aspect of the elementary school curriculum.

Taylor[1] speaks of the need of "bridging engineers" to put to work immediately those principles of creative development about which we already know. This is what I have tried to do these past five years. Working with teachers in workshops and in their own school systems, I have organized those principles stated in the last chapter into teaching acts, and together we have tried to implement creative teaching in all aspects of the school curriculum.

Because the teachers who worked with me were pioneers, creating on the periphery of scientific knowl-

[1] Calvin W. Taylor, "Clues to Creative Teaching," *The Instructor*, June, 1964, p. 5.

edge and subjecting themselves to the principles and techniques discussed in this book, I felt this series of books might serve as guides to all the "bridging engineers" in service and in training. Every example of creative teaching in this volume and in those to follow is written from an actual experience or an observed experience in a classroom.

THE PLACE OF THE CREATIVE ARTS IN RELATION TO CREATIVE DEVELOPMENT

Creativity no longer means dabbling around in the creative arts. It means that we are trying to keep alive those things which nature has given every child to make him a unique individual. It has been a misconception that we teach the creative arts in the elementary school to train artists, composers, and architects. The main purpose of teaching the creative arts in the elementary school is to keep alive the creativity which contributes so much to our democratic way of life.

Although we have associated the development of creativity with the creative arts in the past, the teaching in this area has often done more to "kill off" creativity than to foster it. Art lessons, as such, were often directed to producing a product, drawn like the teacher's and even copied or traced. Children subjected to the gimmicks and patterns of this type of art teaching are now the "painting by numbers" fadists or the cartoon copiers—pathetic in their attempts to achieve aesthetic satisfaction in performing a technical skill rather than a creative act.

Because of our lack of knowledge about creativity and its nurture, the area of the curriculum designated specifically to develop creativity in children often cut it off. The lack of creative people in our modern world and the crying need for them is living testimony to the ineffectiveness of the art, music, and literature teaching of the past. That the objectives of these programs were not met is also obvious in the lack of aesthetic consciousness in our culture today: the vulgarity of our cities, the ugliness of many of our buildings, the worn-out plots and presentations of many of our motion pictures and television programs.

Volume V of this series is devoted to the application of the principles of creative teaching to art and music. It is hoped the changes in method suggested in this book may result in a more creative citizenry and one more sensitive to, appreciative of, and satisfied with the aesthetics of daily life.

THE RELATION OF SCIENCE TEACHING
TO CREATIVE DEVELOPMENT

A great deal of emphasis has been put on science in the past fifteen years. Interest in science is well directed, since we are living in a technological age. Most people, however, think of science in relation to mathematics. Yet science and the creative arts are much more closely allied than science and mathematics when it comes to the actual application of each in the elementary school.

A scientist is one of the most creative persons that our culture can produce. We have said that a person who creates is one who takes old experiences and assembles them into something new, new to him, but not necessarily new to the world. A scientist, on the other hand, is a person who sinks down taps into his past experiences and rearranges them not only into something new to himself but also something new to the world. The same traits which characterize a scientist characterize a creative person. Therefore science and the creative arts go hand in hand and much of the work with children should be directed toward problem-solving, thinking, making judgments, using their own resources, being imaginative and developing a scientific attitude and scientific method.

Volume VII of this series gives many illustrations indicating how the principles of creative teaching may be applied to the teaching of science in the elementary school.

THE RELATION OF THE LANGUAGE ARTS
TO CREATIVE DEVELOPMENT

In the past the emphasis in our schools has been largely placed on "correct" communication rather than clear, imaginative, creative, beautiful, and effective communication. The communication arts have been taught in isolation from the mastery of subject matter, even in isolation from each other. Children read to communicate, they write to communicate, they listen and speak as part of the communication process. This isolation of the language arts from the purposes for which they are taught has often led to a violation of the natural sequence of development, namely: listening, speaking, reading, writing, and those refinements of writing such as word usage, grammar, spelling.

To develop effective, creative communication the language arts must be taught as skills in connection with the subject matter areas so that children are aware of their communicative function and use them as such. *The creative aspects of communication should become the core of the language arts program,* so that children not only develop a skill in the use of the language tools themselves, but a joy and pride in their ability to use the tools of communication for self-expression and self-gratification.

Volume II of this series deals with the application of the creative principles described in this book to listening, oral expression, written expression, handwriting, spelling, grammar, word usage, punctuation, and vocabulary development.

Volume III deals with the application of creative principles to the teaching of reading and literature.

The Relation of the Social Studies
to Creative Development

The Social Studies deal with the greatest problem of man on this planet today: learning to live together. Never before in the history of the world has there been a greater need for creative ways of solving national and international problems. Great thinkers are needed everywhere.

Learning to live together does not just "happen" with the act of growing up. Training is needed to develop in men those qualities and skills essential to successful life in a democratic society. Children must *practice* the act of sharing ideas without acting emotionally, they must *practice* critical and creative thinking, they must *learn* to listen to other people's viewpoints, they must *learn* to use democratic processes and group dynamics, they must *develop* empathy and understanding of people different from them.

The prime reason for the American public school was to take care of all those needs in the functioning of a democratic society which could not be left to chance. One of the first needs was literacy. One need now is learning to live together in peace and harmony. This cannot be left to chance if the world is to survive. We are committed to the development of these skills in children so they function as individuals in a democratic country. In a democracy and in a democracy alone, individuals count, and their rights and freedoms are respected. Creativity is a way of life; democracy is a way of life. Creativity is a state of mind; toleration, empathy, and self-realization are states of mind. Creativity is individualism; democracy is individualism. Creativity functions best in a free society of free thinkers. Our social studies program should be the core for developing the free, creative thinkers of our republic.

Ways this may be done through the application of creative principles is demonstrated in Volume IV of this series. In this book, much attention is given to creative ways of helping children develop values, skills, and understanding, as well as to the creative teaching of social studies content.

The Relation of Mathematics

to Creative Development

It was said not long ago that the laws of mathematics were fixed and unchanging. It was assumed, therefore, that the methods of teaching mathematics must follow suit.

Nothing could have been further from the truth. Never in the history of the American school has there been a change in method so quick, so drastic and so far-reaching as the change in the teaching of mathematics in the elementary schools. In learning mathematics, the elementary school child no longer is asked to remember long lists of facts and rules. He is, instead, placed in the most creative of situations. He goes through the stages of manipulating and exploring materials. He gains insight into concepts and algorisms. He learns through discovery.

Mathematics teaching in today's school contributes to the creative development of children as much as any other area of the curriculum. The creative approach to mathematics is creating not only a generation of literate adults in this area but a generation of critical thinkers and problem solvers as well.

Volume VI of this series is devoted to the application of creative teaching principles to mathematics.

The Relation of Physical Education to Creative Development

One of the most creative books to be published in the past few years is one by Andrews, Saurbourn and Schneider[2] called *Physical Education for Today's Boys and Girls*. It is a significant contribution to creative teaching because it translates into action those conditions necessary to foster creativity in physical education. This is a book with a fresh outlook. It buries alive those dull and stereotyped "gym" periods which placed children in puppet roles, marching and drilling and playing games so highly organized that their needs were more often violated than met. On the grave of such a program blossom the flowers of a new, creative, and wonderful program in physical education. In this new program our knowledge of boys and girls and how they grow and develop is really put to work. The dynamics of growth and development are brought together in a meaningful, comprehensive and clear-cut manner.

Robert S. Fleming[3] in an introduction to this book states:

The creative quality inherent in the teachers' work with children is clearly brought out. But neither physical education nor creativity is treated as an end in itself. The total process is conceived as a means of fostering the total growth of boys and girls . . .

The authors make this statement: "When movement and growth are viewed together they provide a framework for physical education."

[2] Gladys Andrews, Jeanette Saurbourn and Agnes Schneider, *Physical Education for Today's Boys and Girls* (Boston: Allyn and Bacon, 1960).

[3] Robert S. Fleming, *ibid.*, preface.

They proceed to list some basic beliefs about movement education. Among these beliefs they state:

Movement can be an important factor in learning.

Movement experiences can stimulate thinking.

Movement experiences can help children understand their own ideas and feelings.

Movement experiences can help children's understanding of other people.

Movement can be a form of communication.

Movement can provide for self-expression.

Movement education can help children develop social interaction.

Movement education can help children develop physical skills in common and unique activities.

Movement education can provide opportunities for cooperation and competition.

Movement education can help children clarify concepts about their environment.[4]

The text which follows develops these objectives in a creative and exciting manner. A physical education program such as the one described in this book contributes to the creative development of children in every respect.

SUMMARY

The *total* elementary school curriculum supplies the situations, problems, and instances necessary to develop creativity. A referral to the samples of creative teaching described in this book will reveal that "lessons" in the following areas were used to demonstrate creative principles:

The Creative Arts—pages 55–56

The Social Studies—page 161

The Language Arts—pages 16–20

[4] *Ibid.*, p. 7.

To the College Student

Review this book and find instances among the illustrations which show the development of creativity through: oral expression, listening, social studies, writing, construction, audio-visual materials, conversation, human relationships.

Divide your class into small groups. Assign each an area of the elementary school curriculum. Through discussion plan a "lesson" which demonstrates how creativity may be developed through each area. Use as many of the principles of creative teaching as you can. Share your plans with each other. Evaluate them.

Read the quote from Einstein at the introduction of this chapter. What does it mean? Do you agree with it?

Make a list of all the experiences you remember from your art and music classes which you now feel cut down on your creative development.

What are the objectives of teaching art and music in the elementary school? Make a list of all the reasons you think educators feel these two subjects are important to the elementary school curriculum. After the list is finished, check over each item and, using the current adult population as your criterion for judgment, ask yourself whether or not the time and money expended in meeting these objectives has really paid off. Does this suggest that something was wrong in the method of teaching these subjects in the past? What?

To the Classroom Teacher

Review your program for the past week and note in which areas of the curriculum creativity was developed. Then ask yourself if you tend to rely on any one particular area more than others. If so, think of ways you can expand your teaching of creativity to include more subject matter areas.

The statement has been made in this book that often we void what we are trying to accomplish in one area of the elementary school curriculum by the way we teach in another area. A good example of this is a comparison of an art and reading lesson. In a particular art lesson, a teacher was trying to develop freedom of expression and individuality, and copying was not allowed. Only a few minutes after the art lesson, the same teacher taught reading comprehension by having the children use a workbook page on which the exercises said, "Draw three houses like this one. Color one blue." and "Make three balls in these three spaces that look like this ball. Color one red, one yellow, and one blue." Find other inconsistencies in teaching methods and materials of this nature. Can you think of ways reading comprehension (and other skills) might be taught without violating creative principles?

Instead of teaching your students a well-known game, let them try to make up a game. See what happens.

One day encourage your students to present their "Show and Tell" materials through dramatization and gestures rather than through telling.

Here is a list of simple exercises which will evoke creative responses in children. Use them when you have a few extra minutes.

- Be a bowl of jello.

- Show me how it feels to be a cat.

- Act like a watermelon seed.

- Tell me all the ideas that come to your mind when I say "fair."

- What words do you know that are so good they tell exactly what they mean (example: evergreen)?

- What color is happiness?

- Where do the minces come from in mince pie?

To the College Student and
the Classroom Teacher

Consider some of the statements made in this chapter regarding physical education. Keeping them in mind, discuss what part ballet plays in developing creativity in distinction from the part interpretative dance plays in developing creativity.

Make a list of those areas of the curriculum where you feel creativity positively cannot be developed: that is, where convergent thinking processes are the only processes which can be effectively employed.

How is it possible to make each area of the college curriculum an instrument for developing creativity?

Some areas of the curriculum do not appear at first glance to lend themselves to the development of creativity. A list of such areas appears below. Can you think of ways of fostering creativity in each?

- Phonics
- Reading comprehension
- Reading speed
- Handwriting
- Use of the comma
- Spelling
- Correct use of "their" and "there"

List all the ideas you can think of that illustrate how dramatics can develop creativity.

SELECTED BIBLIOGRAPHY

Barkan, M. *Through Art to Creativity*. Boston: Allyn and Bacon, 1960.

Cole, N. *The Arts in the Classroom*. New York: John Day, 1940.

Cosner, E. I. "What is Creativity in the Curriculum?" *Middle School*, LXXV (1960), 22–23.

Drevdahl, J. E. and Cattell, R. B. "Personality and Creativity in Artists and Writers," *Journal Clinical Psychology*, XIV (1958), 107–11.

Guilford, J. P. "Creative Abilities in the Arts," *Psychological Review*, LXIV (1957), 110–18.

Reed, C. H. "Developing Creative Thinking in Arithmetic," *Arithmetic Teacher*, IV (1957), 10–12.

Rubin, L. J. "Creativity and the Curriculum," *Phi Delta Kappan*, XLIV (1963), 438–40.

Strang, R. M. "Creativity in the Elementary Classroom," *National Education Association Journal*, L (March 1961), 20–22.

Wiles, Kimball. *Teaching for Better Schools*, Chapters VI–IX. Englewood Cliffs, N. J.: Prentice-Hall, Inc., 1959.

Wilt, Marion E. *Creativity in the Elementary School*. New York: Appleton-Century-Crofts, Inc., 1959.

Wolfson, B. J. "Creativity in the Classroom," *Elementary English*, XXXVIII (Nov. 1961), 523.

*C reativity in teaching can . . . be judged by the quality
of opportunities actually provided by a teacher for
young people to have educative experiences.*[1]

—ALICE MIEL

[1] Alice Miel, *Creativity in Teaching: Invitations and Instances* (Belmont, California: Wadsworth Publishing Co., Inc., 1961), p. 8.

XI——The Creative Teacher Is You!

THE emerging concepts of creativity reviewed in this book call for attention from all who work with youth. The scientist, the psychologist, the philosopher, the sociologist, the anthropologist, the industrialist, and others, will continue to add to our knowledge of creativity, but with the teachers of America lies the challenge of its nurture. The degree to which they understand the creative concept and are aware of its importance, the degree to which they are willing to search for, experiment with, and apply creative methodology to develop the creative powers of the individual may determine, to a great degree, the fate of this nation. This applies to teachers from nursery school through college. It represents one of the greatest challenges ever presented to the teaching profession!

Can creativity be developed in teachers as we hope to develop it in children? Logic would tell us that the answer is "yes" although research in this area is at present scarce and contradictory. In the last chapter Parnes' work at the University of Buffalo was cited as evidence that creative teaching can be developed.

The implications of the problem are two-fold: it

must be attacked by in-service work with teachers already teaching, and it must be faced in our teacher training institutions as a way of training teachers to teach, or better yet, by a combination of both.

Many universities and teacher-training institutions have already taken steps to meet the problem of training creative teachers. Summer workshops and courses in creative teaching are being offered. Some school systems are affording their teachers in-service programs or courses in creative teaching, using a consultant who is well versed in current research on creativity.

Other school systems are making curriculum changes which include the objective of creative development in all phases of their instructional program. Such changes call for a study of creativity and methods of developing it in children. Such changes also call for new methods, new materials, and a new approach to the teaching act. Such changes also demand new measures of achievement and the inclusion of techniques and devices to measure the development of creativity in the classroom.

In teacher-training institutions, the principles of creativity must apply to the college classroom. As stated in Chapter VII, the concept of teaching must change from that of teaching as a mimetic role to that of teaching as a creative role. Too much of our teacher education today focuses on practicing what we know to be sound educational method. So little of it focuses on what *could* be sound educational method if it were once tried, and subsequently subjected to research.

Young people enter the teaching profession because they feel they have a contribution to make: they envision themselves doing exciting things with children, different from those in their own school experience. Often they are motivated to enter the profession by a successful experience at a summer camp or on a playground. Their success in these situations rightfully gives them the feeling they know how to work with children, and can communicate with them. Then these young people are "put through the mill." They are not shown how *they* can *contribute* to teaching; they are taught what is *known* about teaching and often what is not really known. They are taught what the "experts" think, until they often cannot differentiate between *research in methodology* and *opinion about methodology*. Methods courses, under these circumstances, often become insipid and dull, and fall into disrepute among students.

In accord with new certification requirements, teacher-training programs are placing more and more emphasis on the student teaching experience and the necessity of working with a good cooperating teacher in a public school. Student teachers are graded in these situations largely by their ability to teach *like* the cooperating teacher—again, a mimetic performance rather than a creative one.

Much has been written in the past ten years about teacher education and all its faults. Among the most widely accepted of these writings is Dr. Conant's book, *The Education of American Teachers.*[2] From Dr. Conant's book has come the impetus for the additional emphasis on the student teaching experience. Because young teachers-in-training have seen this as the most practical and realistic of all their experiences, educators and others have gone overboard in recommending more of it. But, it is not *more* of the teaching experience which will effect the necessary changes in developing creative teachers: it is the *nature* and *quality* of the experience. *Not one* of the current publications stresses the fact that the student teaching experience should be a *creative* rather than a mimetic one. All stress the need for placing students with *good* cooperating teachers, and all suggest plans for the proper selection and qualification of these cooperating teachers but none places creativity as a prime requisite for the cooperating teacher.

It is the opinion of this author that, without this necessary requisite, no alteration in program organization in our teacher-training institutions will effect any great change in the products which come from them. The need for *numbers* of teachers to fill the elementary school classrooms of our nation is so great that it is extremely doubtful that enough *creative* cooperating teachers can be currently found with whom to place the young people now in training. The concepts and techniques of creative teaching are too new and too unpracticed to have provided an established backlog of teachers sufficiently skilled in creative methodology to train all the young people now in teacher education. To place the major responsibility of developing creative teachers on the student teaching situation and the cooperating teacher is to permit the teacher-training institution to shirk much of its major responsibility.

[2] James B. Conant, *The Education of American Teachers* (New York: McGraw-Hill Book Company, Inc., 1963).

[189]

It is tragic that in stressing the importance of the student teaching situation, current critics of teacher education have omitted the most important and dynamic element to be considered for substantial and effective change to occur: that creative concepts must be developed in *both* the cooperating teacher and the student teacher. This calls for a cooperative venture in which the college, the public school, and the student work to develop teachers who are unique and individual, and who in turn will allow for uniqueness and individuality in the student teacher. This is the essence of the needed change in teacher education.

Teachers have been goaded too long into following manuals which dictate what they shall say and do every moment of every day. These patterns of teaching must go, and will if basic securities are built through strong self-concepts in the teacher-training institutions.

What Creative Teaching Means

To be creative the teacher must understand that each of the concepts developed in this book applies to her directly. Within her lie her own creative powers; she can begin at once to draw them out. Her attitude toward children must be a wholesome one. She must care about everyday contacts and experiences. She must realize that her teaching does not have to be (actually should not be) like that of her fellow teachers. She will consider creativity a quality for her and her children to nourish together and she will develop methods of open-ended teaching which will provide opportunities for children to grow and develop through sound educational experiences.

The role of the teacher in the creative process is consistently clearer as the various aspects of creativity are explored. The teachers, to develop creativity, must:

1. Set conditions for creativity to develop. This means to provide a desirable physical, emotional, social, and intellectual environment.

2. Teach several skills simultaneously, preferably through demonstration and in meaningful situations so children may bring these skills into play in the creative process.

3. Teach facts in meaningful situations and whenever necessary but also to create situations in which this knowledge may be put to use in problem-solving.

4. Provide rich experiences in every curriculum area. This means teacher-dominated problem-solving and conventional methods of problem-solving are minimized for more challenging ways of creative problem-solving. Learning is more divergent and "open-ended" than convergent and closed.

Torrance[3] states the following behavior is necessary in teachers to establish creative relationships: genuine joy or pride in the creative powers of pupils; the sort of relationship which does much to build self-esteem in individuals; genuine empathy; a creative acceptance of limitations and assets rather than the use of them as vulnerable areas by which to gain control of the individual; a search for the truth about a situation rather than an attempt to impose group consensus or individual opinion; permissiveness; a friendly environment.

None of the above mentioned qualities is impossible to attain. If we believe that people can be educated, and that they can learn, then we must accept the premise that they can learn to be creative. Creative teachers are not necessarily the most talented ones. They have "educated" certain skills and aspects of their personality which others have not.

Teaching is a science and an art. Some people feel that the teacher becomes more and more limited in her field of operation as new theories are tested by research and one method is discovered to be better than another. Research tests theories: it tells us what of our methodology is sound or superior. But it does not tell how to put new knowledge into practice. For instance, research in spelling has told us that the *sight* of the whole word is as important to the child as the vision of each letter. This is knowledge which, combined with our knowledge of the children in our classrooms, should produce positive changes in the *method* of teaching. "How can I make sure my children see the whole word as well as each letter?" the teacher asks. And instead of the oral emphasis used up to this time in her teaching, she thinks up ways she can use a visual emphasis as well. A vocabulary chart appears in the front of the room,

[3] E. P. Torrance, *Guiding Creative Talent* (Englewood Cliffs, N. J.: Prentice-Hall, Inc., 1962), pp. 167–87.

individual word cards are made by the children, she has the children correct their own papers and rewrite misspelled words at once; she uses the words many times in many ways on the chalkboard, she utilizes the pocket chart and the flannel board for spelling exercises and games. Her whole method of teaching has changed.

The *creative teacher* then, is one who takes the new knowledge supplied by the science of education and finds new and practical ways to put it to use in the classroom. She operates on the frontier of educational knowledge—thinking up new ways to implement new knowledge. In doing so, she herself suggests new ideas that need to be scientifically tested. She creates the optimum conditions for learning in her own ways, with her own resources and materials, and for her own children, making her own work an *art*.

Miel[4] says that the products of the teacher's creativity are OPPORTUNITIES for individuals and groups to experience and learn. To create these opportunities, the creative teacher uses ideas of others discretely, and thinks up ideas of her own. She realizes that the potential for solving her teaching problems lies within herself and not in a book written by some person who knows neither her nor the children she teaches.

Zirbes[5] says:

creative teaching is the sensitive insightful developmental guidance which makes learning experiences optimally educative and conducive to the development and fulfillment of the creative potentialities of individuals and groups.

Hughes Mearns[6] defines the creative teacher as the one having the ability to transform others by the contagion of his own peculiar powers. Mearns believes that "no superior outcome is possible . . . without the creative teacher." He states:

She it is whose subtile directing keeps the whole activity going. She shows her admiration for high achievement but honestly and without flattery. She will be patient with the slow worker but she will not give her approval to work that is shoddy. Quite often she will withhold assistance to a child in difficulty, who, she senses, is persisting rewardingly in the right direction. She is sure that being

[4] Miel, *op. cit.*, p. 8.

[5] Laura Zirbes, *Spurs to Creative Teaching* (New York: G. P. Putnam's Sons, 1959), p. 36.

[6] Hughes Mearns, *Creative Power: The Education of Youth in the Creative Arts* (2nd rev. ed.; New York: Dover Publications, Inc.), p. 252 and p. 267.

sensitive he will come through successfully. Her mature use of language, her taste, her confidence in the worth of her work, her genuine interest, all the elements, indeed, that make her an influencing personality—these are at work on the children all the time, although they may never be aware of it.

How often we hear teachers say, "Well, that may be all right for some but I just can't teach that way! I am not creative" or "I just don't believe that all teachers can be creative." Such statements are more indicative of personality problems than of teaching skill. A teacher who recognizes her limited ability to teach creatively can do something about it! To say one cannot teach creatively is to admit one cannot teach. As knowledge increases in any profession, untruths are discarded and truths take their place. Teaching must be no exception. The curriculum content of the future is often fuzzy and unsure. But the future need for creative people is as clear-cut as an algebraic formula. By entering the profession teachers commit themselves to develop the creative potential of every child, and to support the political ideology of the democratic society which needs this potential. If they cannot do this, they had best turn the job over to those who can.

SUMMARY

In his recent book, Calvin Taylor says:

> The development of fully functioning individuals has long been an avowed objective of education. We believe that education in a democracy should help all individuals develop their talents fully— to become as nearly self-actualized as possible. To fully develop the intellectual capacities of our children and to lead them closer to self-actualization, the abilities involved in developing creative thinking and creativity cannot be ignored. The traditional measures of intelligence assess only a few of man's intellectual talents. Man's complex mental operations are not being fully developed or assessed. Among them is his ability to think and act creatively.[7]

Torrance has added other legitimate concerns of education to this one. He states that another goal of the school is healthy personality growth. Although we lack scientifically developed infor-

[7] Calvin Taylor, *Creativity: Progress and Potential* (New York: McGraw-Hill Book Company, 1964), p. 50.

mation concerning the relationships between creativity and mental health, what evidence we do have shows without a doubt that the stifling of creative desires and abilities cuts at the very roots of living and ultimately creates overwhelming tension and breakdown.

Another area related to creativity is educational achievement. Researchers are finding that creative thinking can contribute to the acquisition of information and educational skills. There is a growing body of evidence that creative learning can be more economical and more lasting than learning by authority.

Torrance mentions vocational success as another objective of American education and indicates that creative thinking is important to vocational success even in some of the most common and routine occupations.[8]

Schools are also concerned that their students make useful contributions to the society and to national goals. Toynbee has pointed out that although the United States has been made a great country by a series of creative minorities, we now tend to neglect and suppress such minorities. He warns that the creative minorities and the majority must be sufficiently in tune to establish understanding, confidence, and cooperation between them. The most needed and precious commodity in the world today is creativity. We need not worry about getting men to other planets, about solving problems of racial prejudice, about meeting political crises or about any serious problem if we can learn to direct our energies to the *source* of the solution of all these problems: *the creative mind of man*. In the *creative* mind of man, and there alone, lie the answers to all the problems of all mankind.

The men of tomorrow who must solve these problems and who need these creative attributes are the children of today. They sit before us day after day and within that mass of young minds lies that *potential* force—seething, bubbling, pushing, struggling, and begging to be released in a world that needs it so badly. And, in each mind lies a different ability, a different idea, a different plan.

On the first page of this manuscript Jody, a third grader, asked, "Who am I?" Indeed, who is he? That is what teachers are for—to help him find out who he is, and to help him determine his place in a free society. His education *must* mean that he becomes

[8] E. Paul Torrance, "Education and Creativity" in Taylor, *op. cit.*, pp. 50–56.

the INDIVIDUAL he has the potential of becoming—a human being driven by his own motivations to fulfill his own destiny; one who learns those facts, skills, concepts, and values he *must* to live comfortably with his fellowmen, but one who remains an individual, self-realizing and possessing worth because of his own uniqueness. To be unique he must have developed within him his power to create.

I chose the closing lines of a poem by Robert Frost to introduce this volume—they say well what must be said about the self-actualized, creative person, and it is fitting that I close this book by repeating them:

> Two roads diverged in a wood, and I
> I took the one less traveled by,
> And that has made all the difference.

> Robert Frost[9]

To the College Student and
the Classroom Teacher

In the summer workshop on creativity held at Syracuse University in 1963, the participants, all of whom were classroom teachers, devised the following self-evaluation scale to check their own growth in developing creative concepts. The items on the scale represent the differences this particular group of teachers saw between creative and uncreative teaching. Try checking yourself on this scale: how do you rate?

---

[9] Robert Frost, *You Come Too* (New York: Holt, Rinehart and Winston, 1959), p. 84.

WORKSHOP ON CREATIVITY

SELF-EVALUATION SHEET

Below is a group of characteristics on a continuum which show growth *away* from non-creative toward creative teaching. Place a check on the continuum where you think you are at this stage of your thinking.

THE GROWING, CREATIVE TEACHER MOVES

FROM   TO

1 _____ 10

Rigid over-planned programs   to   flexibility in program

1 _____ 10

An automatic classroom   to   a democratic classroom
atmosphere   atmosphere

1 _____ 10

Convergent thinking   to   divergent-convergent
process   thinking processes

1 _____ 10

Mass instruction   to   ideas for individualized
                                              instruction

1 _____ 10

Thinking of   to   thinking of individuality
conformity   and ways to develop it

1 _____ 10

Planning on the verbal,   to   planning more direct
symbolic level   manipulative-discovery
                                              experiences

1 _____ 10

Seeing creativity as   to   seeing creativity as a
creative arts   quality to be developed
                                              in all areas of curriculum

	FROM		TO
1			10
	Seeing creativity as a talent	to	seeing creativity as an inborn quality which can be drawn out by setting proper conditions in the classroom
1			10
	Seeing creativity as a set of "like" products	to	seeing creativity as individual products—each unique and different
1			10
	Seeing the creative child as a nuisance	to	seeing the creative child as a precious asset
1			10
	Seeing creativity as an expression of a unique talent	to	seeing creativity as the process of decision making, passing judgment, choosing, selecting, perceiving, analyzing, flexibility and fluency of ideas
1			10
	Evaluating children's work as final	to	seeing children's work as a step in the process of creative growth
1			10
	Seeing the curriculum as a means of making junior artists and poets	to	seeing the curriculum as a means to develop creativity
1			10
	Seeing creativity as a frill to the curriculum; an addition	to	seeing creativity as the core to the curriculum; an essential to inspired learning
1			10
	Stressing competition	to	stressing cooperation

FROM		TO
1		10
Seeing creativity as a frill	to	seeing creativity as a method of teaching
1		10
Making plans by herself	to	involving children in planning
1		10
Teaching in isolated class periods	to	integrating curriculum: unit teaching
1		10
Stereotyped conformity	to	free expression and a willingness to try new ideas
1		10
Passive compliance	to	active identification
1		10
Imposed direction	to	cooperative planning
1		10
Extrinsic motivation	to	intrinsic value concerns
1		10
Submissive acquiescence	to	wholehearted involvement
1		10
Restrictive domination	to	responsible self-direction
1		10
Harmful suppression	to	spontaneity
1		10
Fixed ways of thinking, fixed skills	to	more flexible response to teaching situations

Now that you have read this book, what items would you add to this scale?

SELECTED BIBLIOGRAPHY

Alexander, William M. *Are You a Good Teacher?* New York: Rinehart and Company, Inc., 1959.

Anderson, Harold H. (ed.). *Creativity and Its Cultivation.* New York: Harper and Brothers, 1959.

Ashton-Warner, Sylvia. *Spinster.* New York: Simon and Schuster, 1959.

———. *Teacher.* New York: Simon and Schuster, 1963.

Barron, F. "The Disposition Toward Originality," *Journal of Abnormal Psychology,* No. 3 (1951), 478–85.

Beauchamp, George A. *Basic Dimensions of Elementary Method.* Boston: Allyn and Bacon, 1959.

Bixler, J. S. "An Experiment in Undergraduate Thinking," *Bulletin American Association of University Professors,* XLIII (1957), 282–87.

Bruner, J. S. *On Knowing.* Cambridge: Belknap Press, 1962.

Bulletin of Bureau of School Service: Creativity and College Teaching, XXXV, No. 4. Lexington: College of Education, University of Kentucky, 1962.

Byers, Loretta and Irish, Elizabeth. *Success in Student Teaching.* Boston: D. C. Heath and Company, 1961.

Crawford, Robert P. *The Techniques of Creative Teaching.* New York: Hawthorne Books, Inc., 1954.

Department of Classroom Teachers, *Conditions of Work for Quality Teaching.* Washington, D. C.: The National Education Association, 1959.

Dunkel, H. B. "Creativity and Education," *Educational Theory,* XI (Oct. 1961), 209–16.

Getzels, Jacob W. and Philip W. Jackson. *Creativity and Intelligence.* New York: John Wiley and Sons, Inc., 1962.

Haefele, W. *Creativity and Innovation.* New York: Reinhold, 1962.

Harrison, Raymond H. and Gowin, Lawrence E. *The Elementary Teacher in Action.* San Francisco: Wadsworth Publishing Company, Inc., 1958.

Lane, Howard and Beauchamp, Mary. *Human Relations in Teaching.* Englewood Cliffs, N.J.: Prentice-Hall, 1955.

Logan, Lillian and Logan, Virgil G. *Teaching the Elementary School Child.* Boston: Houghton Mifflin Company, 1961.

MacKinnon, Donald W. "What Makes a Person Creative?" *Saturday Review,* X (Feb. 1962), pp. 5–7.

Maslow, A. H. "Cognition of Being in the Peak-experiences," *Journal of Genetic Psychology,* LXXXIV (March, 1959), 43–66.

Smith, Paul (ed.). *An Examination of the Creative Process.* New York: The Hastings House, Publishers, Inc., 1959.

Stein, Morris I. and Heinze, Shirley. *Creativity and the Individual.* Glencoe, Illinois: The Free Press, 1960.

Vander Werf, Lester S. *How to Evaluate Teachers and Teaching.* New York: Rinehart and Company, Inc., 1958.

─────Index